HIDE and SEEK

HIDE and SEEK

A Wartime Childhood

Theresa Cahn-Tober

University of New Mexico Press
Albuquerque

Library of Congress Cataloging-in-Publication Data

Cahn-Tober, Theresa.
Hide and seek : a wartime childhood / Theresa Cahn-Tober.
p. cm.
Originally published: New York, NY : Harmony Press, 2002.
ISBN 0-8263-3198-X (pbk. : alk. paper)
1. Jewish children in the Holocaust—Poland—Biography.
2. Jews—Poland—Biography.
3. Holocaust, Jewish (1939-1945)—Poland
—Personal narratives.
4. Righteous Gentiles in the Holocaust—Poland.
5. Poland—Biography.
I. Title.
DS135.P63 C34 2003
940.53'18'092—dc21
2003005063

Printed and bound by Edwards Brothers, Inc.

Typeset in Sabon 11.5/16; Display type
set in Willow ITC and Futura Condensed

Photographs courtesy of author

Design and composition: Robyn Mundy

1 2 3 4 5 6 7 8 9 10

To my grandchildren
Jeremy, Carmel, and Sarah

CONTENTS

INTRODUCTION

· · · · · · · · · · · · · · · · · ·

> To write one must have memories . . . and still that is not enough. One must be able to forget them and . . . wait 'til they come again. For it is not yet the memories themselves. Not 'til they have turned to blood within us . . . can it happen that . . . the first word arises.
>
> —Rainer Maria Rilke

"What is your name?" a new acquaintance asked the other day, and I paused a moment to think. "That's not a trick question," the man laughed, and I laughed along so as not to appear crazy. The fact is that at one time this was indeed a trick question—and it could have tricked me out of my life. Years later it still stirs up a feeling, an extra intake of breath, a need, as it were, to gather my selves together.

What is your name? Where are you from? What is your religion? Who are your parents? How old are you? The answers to these simple questions, which any three-year-old can rattle off, once formed a complex code on which my very survival depended. They changed, during my childhood, with dizzying frequency. At a moment's notice, I could don a new name, age, religion, and family affiliation. Surviving the Holocaust in hiding required that the self I was at one moment could transform into another at the next.

What I could always be sure of as a child is that I was hiding. Hiding behind a china closet, in an attic, a basement, a convent. Hiding with my beloved Marysia, with the nuns, with the countess, with farmers and strangers. Hiding from Nazis, Poles, from Christians, and even from other Jews. Hiding from bombs. Hiding my body, my identity, my beliefs and feelings. And in the silence of my own soul, seeking who I really was.

In a deadly game of hide and seek, the evil unleashed by Hitler hunted for, and most often found, children huddled in their hiding places. I was one of the very few to escape. My gratitude to those who hid me—and, consequently, had to hide themselves—wraps me as closely as my skin. It never leaves my awareness. There were many Poles who helped me survive, and to them all I am grateful. But the courage and compassion shown by Marysia, whom you will soon meet, daily fills me with awe.

Like many Holocaust survivors, I often ask myself, "Why me?" Why did I survive when so many others died? And what obligation do I have to fulfill?

Though there is no answer to why I survived, I think I know my obligation: I survived as a child, and so I must work to prevent violence from hunting and hurting children. As a clinical psychologist, I have spent the last thirty-five years helping families to live in greater harmony, protecting children from abuse, seeking ways to heal emotional wounds inflicted on children by adults—and sometimes by their peers. Most recently, I worked for five years on the Navajo reservation, creating a program for victims of domestic violence and leading groups for children from violent homes. I listened as eight- and nine-year-old Indian youngsters told of having to hide—under the bed, in the doghouse, in the hogan of a distant relative, alone in a boarding school. I listened as they told of hiding their terror and their tears. And I saw myself, a small girl behind a china closet.

I offer this story of my childhood as a small token of gratitude to my rescuers, their children and grandchildren. Equally dear to my heart is the wish to share with you or perhaps to remind you, what it is like for a child to live in fear. For only when we truly absorb this can we build a world in which no child has to hide.

NOTE

I have been asked how I can remember events that occurred when I was so young. Although I do remember a great deal, my memory has been supplemented by that of my parents and the sons of my rescuer, Marysia, whom I call my brothers. In addition, I have returned to Poland several times in recent years to revisit the places where I lived. I have also dipped into my imagination to fill in details of certain situations and specifics of dialogue. In all cases what I have written is emotionally true, though perhaps not always factually accurate. This must be the case with any attempt to reconstruct the past.

The vast majority of names in the book are real, particularly the names of the major "characters," such as my family, my rescuers, and the countess. The false names that we all used in hiding are also "real." Since my memory failed, I did have to create names for the villagers in Mstow, the sisters at the convent, and several other "minor players."

CHAPTER ONE

. . . .

Make-Believe

Things happen in life so fantastic that no
imagination could have invented them.
—Isaac Bashevis Singer

Even in the bomb shelters, my father loved to tell stories.
I was five then, hiding from Adolf Hitler and his Nazi
German forces in the Polish city of Lvov. The relative safety
of the Russian occupation of Poland was ending. Hitler had
just broken his "non-aggression" pact with Joseph Stalin, the
leader of Russia and the rest of the Soviet Union. As Hitler
chased the Russians from eastern Poland, Lvov reeled under
a ceaseless rain of bombs. The year: 1941.

● ● ● ● ●

Sirens rip the air, warning of a raid by German bomber planes. The tenants of our building dash down to the interconnected network of basements that serve as shelters. We file in silently, like ghosts, huddling in the dim, dank underground. Mama ushers me and Babcia, my maternal grandmother, to a bench. I slide in next to Hanka, my four-year-old friend from next door. Her mother, Janina, crouches beside us on the damp floor. Her long blond hair, usually neatly braided and arranged in a crown, hangs loosely over her bathrobe. Janina's husband—dark, intense—circles the cellar in short, nervous steps. His fingers travel along the crumbling plaster, patting down the weakest parts. The janitor and his wife peer out of their basement apartment.

Rushing in last is my seventeen-year-old Uncle Artur, out of breath, dressed smartly for a date. I barely control myself from running to him, having him twirl me around until my head spins. But I know I must keep quiet. I wave to him; he doesn't notice. He has a girlfriend now and wears a dreamy expression even as the sirens wail. I shift my gaze to the other neighbors, a dozen or so, many of whom I have never met. They settle down, or mill around with somber faces, as the first bombs blast the silence.

During the heavy, fearful pauses between bombs, my father entertains. The weak flicker of the kerosene lamp plays on his mobile features as he warms to his tale.

"Before the war," he begins, focusing on me, though others are listening, "when you were very little . . ."

To me, "before the war" was make-believe—once upon a time.

"Before the war, we had oranges for breakfast."

A neighbor chuckles. Even staple foods have become scarce. Meat, eggs, butter, and fruit have been replaced by stored potatoes, flour, and lard. Rumor has it that one of our neighbors recently ate her dog.

"What are oranges?" I ask.

"An orange is . . . like a potato," my father explains, groping for concepts I'll understand. "It tastes sweet, like bread with sugar."

He cups his hands around the imaginary fruit, then digs his nails into the skin to peel it. The invisible juice squirts out and he winces in mock surprise. He jumps up, shakes his shirt, and calls my mother to wipe off the golden drops. My mother starts to oblige but gets distracted by the lice crawling in the seam of his collar. She squashes them expertly between her thumbnails.

Another bomb. The basement shakes, but nothing caves in. The kerosene lantern wavers and then regains its balance. His chain of thought broken, my father starts anew.

"Before the war," he muses, "I was the most respected doctor in Katowice." He scratches absentmindedly where the lice have lodged. "Your mother wore the finest furs, tailored by the best . . ."

I pretend to believe him, like children humor their parents about Santa Claus.

"Before the war" stories. I heard them many times. My father would launch into one with the least provocation. My favorites were subtitled "When you were very little . . ." or "When you were born . . ."

"The day you were born, three years before the war, your mother and I were preparing for a party."

It was Mama's birthday, and they had been invited to celebrate with friends.

From the fourth-story window of their apartment in Katowice, they could see the high drifts of snow sparkling under the gas streetlamps. It was February 1936, and the usual frigid Polish winter. In a rare lapse of professional responsibility, my father—I called him Tatus (Ta' toosh)—left his office early, canceling his appointments with the last two patients and leaving his nurse to deal with their complaints. This gesture, plus a crystal vase of fragrant roses, signaled my father's resolve to dispel the smoggy atmosphere still hovering from an earlier argument.

Here my mother sometimes broke into the story: "Yes, we had had a fight, but I wanted to enjoy my birthday. So I forgave him," she said with a smile.

My father quickly reclaimed the floor: "Mama helped me choose my wardrobe. You know I'm helpless when it comes to fashion."

With his famous memory for detail, he recalled the white shirt, polka-dotted tie, brown broad-striped suit with a vest. Completing her own toilette, Mama plucked her eyebrows, dusted her cheeks with loose powder, and applied a bright crimson lipstick.

Ready to leave, Tatus reached into the hall closet for Mama's mink coat. Though amply cut, it now barely covered her belly; I was due to be born in two weeks.

As she started to slip her arms into the sleeves, she suddenly bent over in pain. Labor had begun, and their plans had to change. Tatus rushed downstairs to whistle for a cab—a horse-drawn sleigh. They sped silently over the snow toward the hospital. The birthday party went on without its guest of honor. My mother, however, received a surprise birthday gift.

It was not much of a prize. I was bald. My eyes traveled in separate directions. I refused to accept Mama's breast. After one day of fruitless effort, she transferred the responsibility for my nourishment to Miss Anna, a nanny whom I would come to hate.

They named me Irena Stefania Licht. My mother liked Irena; my father preferred Stefania. Perhaps he had been hoping for a Stefan, though he always claimed that it was only my mother who had wanted a boy.

Contrary to usual Jewish practice, I was not named for a deceased relative. In their efforts to assimilate—to fit into the larger society—my parents avoided drawing attention to their religion. The local rabbi did convince them to assign me an additional Jewish name. "In case of a religious ceremony, when such a name would be required," he explained. They agreed on Gittle, after my father's deceased mother. However, my parents never attended Jewish ceremonies. They shunned synagogues. The name Gittle was never used; it was a phantom name. I was Irena Stefania Licht (Irenka, Irenia, Irusia, sometimes Kit-kit). It was a name I was destined not to carry for long.

● ● ● ● ●

Mama, Tatus and me.

My knack for interfering with my parents' plans pre-dated my birth. Still childless after three years of marriage, they had booked passage on a cruise to Sweden and Finland. The fee, stiff and unrefundable, had to be paid months in advance. Shortly before the August departure, my mother woke to a morning of nausea—my first bid for attention.

Naturally, the voyage was out of the question, for Mama at least. Undaunted, Tatus, with the resourcefulness that would serve him well in the coming years, proposed a solution: He would sail with his sister Berta, while Mama stayed home with the maid. The proposal was met with choked silence, which Tatus chose to take for assent. In the ensuing weeks, which marked the travel preparations as well as the voyage itself, my mother's anger pulsated through the placenta.

Back from the voyage—suntanned, bursting with stories—my father greeted my mother with a peace offering: a hand-embroidered negligee crafted, Swedish folk-style, from soft cotton cloth. Mama's long-restrained resentment exploded. Cotton? Only peasants wear cotton, and then only to milk cows! She deserved nothing less than silk. With the negligee slung over her arm, Mama stormed into the kitchen, where Zosia, the maid, was preparing dinner.

"The Doctor brought you a present," she announced, and returned to the living room empty-handed.

The incident was never mentioned again—and never forgotten. It remained in my mother's bag of bargaining chips, the sort that couples use to negotiate their balance of power.

Tatus returned to Mama's good graces by arranging another trip, more exotic even than the first. I was just a few weeks old when my parents set out for two months abroad. This time I did not interfere. I remained home with Aunt Berta, the culprit who had usurped my mother's place on the cruise.

Perhaps due to this early bonding, Aunt Berta became a great love of my life. Her rare visits, which included my two teenage cousins, were always a celebration. Aunt Berta sported a soft bosom, which cushioned her enthusiastic hugs. She laughed a lot and had my father's gift for performance. She enthralled me with dramatic enactments of my favorite fairy tales. Her face, folded into wrinkles, danced as she

Aunt Berta and me, 1937.

assumed different identities. With facial expressions as flexible as my father's, she could metamorphose from a waif to a witch, from a princess to a pirate, in an instant. I watched in awe and terror as sweet Little Red Riding Hood turned into a savage wolf. I could swear I saw the grandma's body wiggle inside him, while Aunt Berta's stomach twitched and trembled to the accompaniment of ferocious growls emanating from behind a wicked grin. And then the grandma emerged unharmed—old, tottering, barely able to stand. But now Aunt Berta switched to "Hansel and Gretel." She pulled me out of bed to sing and dance "Brother, come and dance with me." And when we tumbled back on the bed from exhaustion, my full-bodied aunt huffing and puffing, she reached into her shopping bag for gingerbread cookies, purportedly brought directly from Hansel and Gretel's house, sparkling with bits of colorful marzipan.

Once, only once, before the war, did I get a chance to travel to Aunt Berta's home in faraway Przemysl. Her daughters' room was a replica of the same gingerbread house! When it was time to leave, I cried. My parents promised we would soon return.

But by the next time I visited Aunt Berta, a lot had changed.

•　•　•　•　•

The three years of my life before the war still seem like make-believe. They have largely slipped into oblivion. Yet I remember Aunt Berta's joyful spirit. And other memories occasionally spring into brilliant focus, like the pictures in the "Magic Eye." When you first look at these pictures, you see only meaningless scribbles. But when you relax your gaze and focus far in the distance, a vibrant, three-dimensional scene blossoms from the page.

We are getting ready for a walk, just my father and I; no mother today, and no nanny. I am two. Tatus follows me down the stairs, which I maneuver cautiously, the same foot always in the lead, my hand tightly grasping the banister. (My

I'm three years old. Just before the war.

fearfulness frustrates Mama. "I forbid you to be afraid!" she says when I tremble before a sidewalk curb.) Tatus is carrying my doll carriage and, inside it, my doll Pavelek. This is a very special event. Generally Mama refuses to take out the carriage. It's too heavy to lug down three flights of steps, she says. I can play with it at home. But now Tatus is carrying the carriage, swinging it around easily, as if it weighed nothing at all.

On the sidewalk he helps me to arrange Pavelek under a blue satin cover. Pavelek is my favorite doll. He has a round, pink-cheeked porcelain face, and blue eyes that open and close. His head is bald.

Chapter 1

My father taking me for a walk.

Make-Believe

I strut proudly next to Tatus, wheeling the carriage. He stops every few minutes to tip his hat to an acquaintance, exchange a few words, kiss a lady's hand. "Good morning, Doctor," they greet him. "Good morning, Irenka," they say to me.

I say nothing. I am shy.

Tatus lingers with a couple of friends, and I stroll on ahead. Absorbed in my role as Pavelek's mommy, I hardly notice that my father is no longer beside me. Finally aware, I turn around, expecting him to be following behind.

The street is empty. I search in every direction. No Tatus. My lip begins to quiver. "Tatus, Tatus," I call, tears flowing.

Suddenly, like a rabbit from a hat, my father springs out of a doorway. He was hiding. "Here I am," he laughs, rubbing his hands at the joke. "Did you think I would leave you, Kit-kit?" I gasp through laughter and tears.

We continue our walk. This time I push the doll carriage with one hand. With the other, I clutch my father's pants.

●　●　●　●　●

He comes home from work, jingling his pockets. I run to greet him. As he leans forward, I plunge my hand into the inside pocket of his jacket. Only keys. He wiggles away, jiggles the front pocket with the big flap. I grope for that one. Coins. Finally, in the deep pants pocket that slants way down, I find the prize: a handful of sourballs. When I grow up, I want to be a man, with a multitude of pockets.

●　●　●　●　●

My nanny, Miss Anna, is a woman of great patience. She can spend hours feeding me spinach. Spinach, according to my father, is essential for healthy children. He is a pediatrician; his word is law.

Miss Anna and I engage in a daily power struggle. Long after my parents have left the table, we remain seated, with my plate of spinach untouched. Miss Anna manages to sneak a spoonful into my mouth the moment I relax my guard. Or else she pushes the spoon with determination between my clenched lips. Even then, though, the battle is not lost. I form a clump of spinach and saliva and deposit it inside the pouch of my cheek. The clump sits there. Usually Miss Anna gives up before I do, and files a report with my mother.

In addition to spinach and Miss Anna, I hate bedtime. My father tries to ease the way with a story. Unlike his sister, who enacts popular fairy tales, Tatus creates his own. "Once upon a time . . . king and queen . . . little princess . . . a palace full of toys and candy (I close my eyes, picturing the happy scene) . . . suddenly a giant monster breaks through the door (I open my eyes, terrified) . . . with the magic seed, the princess chases away (I relax again) . . . .uh-oh, the monster is climbing in through the chimney (I shiver) . . . happily ever after." I fall asleep.

* * * * *

But some evenings with Tatus were different:

"Tatus will tuck you in later," Mama says.

I'm almost three.

"Is he with patients?" I ask, scooting under the cozy goose-down cover.

"Yes," Mama laughs. I wait, tingly, for our goodnight game. She bends down toward me.

"Nine," I remind her as she puckers her lips. "You promised."

She remembers: 1, 2, 3 . . . 4, 5, 6 . . . 7, 8, 9. Three groups of three kisses make nine. I can already count to ten.

"Nine more," I beg. "Just today."

She wrinkles her brow in a mock scowl. "A deal's a deal." We settle on six.

"Goodnight, Kit-kit," she says. "Remember your promise. Tatus will be surprised."

My hands curl into fists. "I promise I won't suck my thumb."

It's hard to fall asleep. When Tatus comes home, my thumb still imprisoned in my fist, I can hardly wait to show him. I listen for his footsteps. But instead, I hear another fight.

"Stupid! Idiot! How many times did I . . ." His voice rises to a screech.

"Quiet, the child is sleeping," Mama whispers.

Now I cannot make out the words. Something crashes. *Psia krev!* Tatus curses. "Dog's blood!" Mama's voice has vanished. Is she dead? My thumb flies into my mouth.

• • • • •

Once upon a time. Was there really a time before the war? Did our family in Katowice really exist?

A few photos survived to bear witness. One, which later got lost, shows my father in a relaxed, confident pose. His tweed coat falls casually open, revealing the formal suit and tie that befitted his station as a prominent physician. He dominates the space. Slightly behind him, my mother, the "Frau Doctor," stands regal and self-contained, her hands submerged in the pockets of a sleek coat, richly trimmed with fur. A matching fur hat frames her beautiful face. Her black eyes, shaped like almonds, are set in smooth, olive-tone skin. I stand between them, squeezed stiffly into a charming little coat whose collar and sleeves are, like my mother's, trimmed with fur. My arms stick out to the sides like the handles of a corkscrew. I look weary of the struggle with the nanny, who dressed me too snugly and properly for this ritual stroll with my parents.

My parents smile into the camera with grace and composure, like a king and queen, certain of their glorious future. So certain, in fact, that Hitler's invasion of Poland took them completely by surprise.

CHAPTER TWO

Babcia the Bourgeois

Sometime they'll give a war and nobody will come.
—Carl Sandburg

War exploded on September 1, 1939. The Soviet Union and Nazi Germany agreed to split Poland between them. Western Poland, including our hometown, Katowice, fell to the Germans. Within days of the German invasion, the Nazis began rounding up Jews and shooting them in public squares. I heard the word "Jews" mentioned repeatedly now, usually in hushed tones.

At age three, however, I didn't know that it had anything to do with me. Somewhere I had gathered that a Jew was an old man with a long beard. Once, before the war, I had spotted such an oldster limping along across the street.

My *maternal*
grandmother, Babcia.

"Is that a Jew, Mama?" I asked.

"Yes," she replied, and said no more.

I didn't know that I was a Jew or that being a Jew was dangerous, but it didn't take me long to absorb the terror hanging in the air. And then the terror entered our own home. Late one evening, two German SS men, with their infamous big boots and thunderous voices, pounded on our door. I watched from my bed, clutching Pavelek, as they marched my father away.

"Just to answer questions," Mama reassured me. "He'll be back soon."

But she rolled a cigarette with shaking hands and drew in deep gulps of smoke. I popped my thumb in my mouth.

In the middle of the night, my father returned. I woke from a half-sleep to hear: "They shot all the others." He was released because he was a doctor. The Nazis thought he could be useful to them. Relieved, I went back to sleep.

My parents needed no further warnings. They decided to escape while travel was still possible. And so we took off for Lvov, where my grandmother, Babcia, owned an apartment house. Lvov, in eastern Poland, was occupied by the Russians. No one there loved them, but at least they were not killing Jews, like the Nazis were.

The Russians hired my father to treat sick railroad workers. He often had to travel to various locations. These trips were just the first of many separations to come during the course of the war.

Babcia occupied a large, sunny apartment on the third floor of her building. A flower-bedecked balcony looked out on Piekarska Street. Widowed twice, she lived with her seventeen-year-old son Artur, my mother's half-brother.

Uncle Artur wore a crewcut and a big grin. When we first arrived, he had not yet acquired his girlfriend. He loved to play with me, tossing me in the air, whirling me around, pretending he was a scary bear. In the tense and somber atmosphere of those days, he was a whiff of fresh air.

My mother adored her half-brother, who was fifteen years her junior. As a teenager she had often fed, diapered, and bathed him, or simply kept the active toddler out of Babcia's hair. Babcia welcomed the help, not being particularly maternal herself. A handsome woman, conscious of the charms that had attracted two husbands, Babcia—

much like my father—enjoyed spinning stories. Hers focused on her earlier fortunes, on the two husbands who had treated her like a queen.

The building left to her by her second husband had once been a source of pride. Now it had become a liability. It stamped her as a "Bourgeois." In line with the Communist philosophy of the Russians occupying this part of Poland, the term included anyone with a higher education as well as all property owners. The Bourgeoisie must be eliminated—or, at least, stripped of their social and economic status. According to the Communists, the world now belonged to the workers, the Proletariat.

Shortly after our arrival in Lvov, a Russian soldier in a sloppy brown uniform barged into the apartment. He waved a sheaf of official papers in my grandmother's face.

"You are to vacate your apartment by tomorrow morning," he announced. "Comrade Malewski, the janitor, will move in here. You will move into his quarters down in the cellar."

He left. Moments later, the janitor knocked diffidently on the door. The Russian had already paid him a visit.

"Mrs. Zimand," he said to my grandmother, "what would my wife and I do in this big apartment? We are used to our comfortable space in the basement. We don't want to change with you."

And so the change did not take place. A few weeks later, however, the Russians got wind of the fact that my grandmother, the Bourgeois, had not yet been brought low. Another Russian soldier, also armed with papers, appeared at our door.

"Here are my orders," he told Babcia. "You and your family will be deported to Russia."

Unlike the Germans, the Russians would tolerate an argument. While Babcia stood in stunned silence, my mother rose to the challenge.

"What do you mean?" she confronted the soldier in a voice more authoritative than I had ever heard before. "My husband, my mother's son-in-law, is working for the People. He is curing sick railroad workers."

"These are the orders," the Russian insisted. "They are written right here." He tried to decipher the papers, but he was illiterate and could not make them out. Flustered, he stuck the papers behind his back.

"Who is your superior?" my mother asked.

His face flushed, but before he could express his anger, my mother shifted to a softer approach.

"You look tired," she said. "How about a little vodka?"

She offered him a comfortable chair. He sank into it gratefully. Before the third shot of vodka was down, my mother had the name of the superior. She rushed off to see him as soon as the soldier, waving cheerfully, left. The superior accepted her argument. The deportation order was canceled.

For the next few weeks, life proceeded more or less uneventfully. Babcia and Mama traveled to nearby farms to purchase food. Farmers could be bribed, with extra money or jewelry, to sell their dwindling stores of chicken, eggs, and butter. What went for beef often turned out to be horse meat. Pig fat—lard—was easier to come by than butter, but Babcia refused to bring it into her home. Eating pork is forbidden to Jews, she insisted. My father objected: "There's a war! You think God wants us to starve?" But Babcia held her ground. She maintained her Jewish practices in every way possible. When she lit candles on Shabbat, she began to teach me about my faith. But the candles were lit behind drawn curtains, and I wondered why the beautiful rituals that defined my identity needed to be shrouded in secrecy.

My father shuttled back and forth between us and his job. At home, he more and more frequently raged at my mother: The soup was too watery, the salt left off the table, she was inattentive to his stories, she had forgotten to iron his shirt. His temper sizzled throughout the apartment. My mother explained that "Tatus is nervous."

Only my cheerful Uncle Artur could ease the tension. By now madly in love, he floated around the house singing his favorite tune:

I invited my honey to meet me at nine,
Now I'll ask the boss
For a little advance
To buy her red roses and take her to dine
In the charming café where we'll eat, drink, and dance.
And after the movies, we'll stroll and we'll spoon,
Under the brilliant glow of the moon.
Joy and delight will fill my whole heart
Until the sun rises and says we must part,
And again I will ask her to meet me at nine.
Again and again—that hour is fine.

Uncle Artur with me in 1936.

His singing and laughter coaxed smiles out of my mother in those days when not much else did. But she was fated to carry his image in a heavy sack of guilt.

"I wish I had never argued with the Russians about the deportation," she would often cry in later years. "If we had gone to Russia, maybe my brother would still be alive." Because two years later, the Germans invaded the rest of Poland. And they murdered Uncle Artur in Janowska concentration camp.

CHAPTER THREE

Behind the China Closet

"It's awfully hard to be b-b-brave," said Piglet,
"when you are only a
Very Small Animal."
—A. A. Milne

Lvov, 1941. As the German bombers continued to fight the Russians, our constant descents into the gloomy basement shelters dampened even my father's spirits. He told fewer and fewer stories. I tried to play with little Hanka, but our hearts were not in it. Mostly I sat still, silent, or fell into an exhausted sleep on my mother's lap.

Finally, the bombing stopped. The Russians were forced out. The Germans, from whom we had escaped in 1939, now began hounding the Jews in Lvov. All Jews must wear an armband with a yellow Star of David, they proclaimed. In a random fashion, Nazi soldiers barged into homes to "select" Jews for roundups. The roundups were called *Akcia*, "Actions."

Our Christian neighbor in the building, Janina, had relatives in the Polish underground. They informed her in advance when an Action was imminent. She would knock three times on our connecting wall to warn us.

I'm taking Pavelek for a stroll.

Chapter 3

Janina was married to a Jew. He had just escaped and was probably in hiding somewhere in Russia, she thought. She hoped that people there would help him like she was helping us.

· · · · ·

My parents have prepared our hiding place. When news of the next Action reaches us, we spring into a well-practiced routine. Mama knocks three times on the connecting wall to alert Janina that we are ready. Janina peeks out of her front door, checks the hall, the stairway, listens for footsteps. Then she steals softly into our apartment. Meanwhile, we gather a few possessions to help pass the time; who knows how long we'll be in hiding? Mama grabs her silver cigarette case, with the tobacco on one side and delicate rolling papers on the other. Tatus pockets two decks of cards. I gently lift Pavelek from his doll carriage. "Don't be afraid," I mouth to him, wordlessly. I seldom speak out loud anymore. The sound of my own voice startles me. "Don't be afraid, Pavelek."

We head for the kitchen. A tall china closet blocks the door to our hidden shelter. My parents push the closet aside, and we file into a small room with an adjoining toilet. It used to serve as a maid's room before the war. Now it holds two folding chairs, a bridge table, a radio. Two mattresses stand propped against the wall. Extra supplies are piled in a corner: changes of clothes, blankets, a first-aid kit, a flashlight.

Tatus closes the door. With the windows shut and shuttered, the small room, now bulging with four stow-aways, feels airless. I stifle the urge to cough. From the other side of the door we hear Janina shoving the china closet back in place.

Janina tiptoes away. Later, after dark, she will return with a pot of potato stew.

We settle in. Tatus switches on the radio, the volume barely audible. Possibly the underground station reports news of the Action. I cuddle Pavelek, then play school with my fingers. Each finger has a name and personality. Some are well behaved, like the pinky; some naughty, like the thumb; some shy, like the ring finger. I am the teacher and order them around. Usually this game is reserved for bedtime, or else for escape when my parents argue. My fingers take the place of the brothers and sisters I wish I had.

Suddenly the front doorbell rings, insistently, without a pause. It screams like an air-raid siren. We hold our breaths. I have to go to the bathroom, but I know we must be totally silent now. I'm afraid I will wet my pants. The bell keeps ringing and ringing forever. Finally, it stops. I hear heavy boots pound along the outside hallway. Then nothing. It's quiet. We wait. I cross my legs.

The boots return and we can hear a key turn in the lock. Apparently the janitor has been summoned to open the door. The door slams. Boots thunder inside our home. They advance toward the kitchen. I cover my mouth and my nose to silence my breathing. The china closet vibrates to the stomp of the boots. I grasp my mother's hand. She pulls me closer and I can feel her shake. I glance at Babcia. She is silently moving her lips. Her head shakes with the tremor she gets when she's upset.

Chapter 3

My father catches my eye and makes a funny face. He cocks his head, wrinkles his nose and forehead, and stretches his lips in a clown smile. I smile back to please him.

The boots recede. The china closet stops trembling. Now we hear dresser drawers tearing open, smashing on the floor in the bedrooms. Closet doors bang against the wall. Clothes hangers jangle. Guttural voices spew growls that I don't understand.

"They're taking my furs," my mother whispers.

"Shh!" Tatus snaps. The clown face is gone. He looks furious now, and frightened.

The front door finally slams behind the intruders. Tatus reassures us: It's a reasonable bet that they won't return today. We all look to him to assess events. His features relax. I figure it's safe now to use the toilet—though not yet to flush. We must hide quietly until the Action is called off.

Mama rolls a cigarette. She takes deep drags. The already stuffy room fills with smoke. Babcia coughs.

Tatus lays out the cards. My parents play *krapet*, a form of double solitaire, on the bridge table. Tatus puffs occasionally on Mama's cigarette. The danger of his anger has passed for now.

Through the slats in the shutters we see daylight dimming, then dying. Janina drags the china closet back just enough to sneak in a pot of stew. A breath of fresh air filters into the room before she seals us in again. We eat in the dark. My mother pulls down the mattresses for us to rest.

In the morning I wake up in my own bed. The Action was over at midnight.

• • • • •

For me, the Actions paled in comparison to the daily battles at home. My father's attacks on my mother sprang out of nowhere, triggered by nothing at all. It could be a misplaced piece of paper, inadequate seasoning in the soup, inattention to his stories, her voice too loud for safety or too soft to be easily heard, a slight disagreement with his opinion, failure to react fast enough to his requests. A friendly, joking mood would suddenly skid into irritation. He struck her only with words, but for me these might as well have been fists. At times he pounded his own head, smacked his chest, hinted at a heart attack. "You will walk on my grave!" he threatened Mama, and sometimes Babcia, who could also be the target of his wrath.

Not I. He never yelled at me. I was "the child," not worthy of his angry passion. Yet I raged against him, silently, of course. Inside, I took my mother's part. If only she would stand up to him! But she just shriveled into herself.

"Tatus is nervous," she would say, as if this excused his outbursts.

Another argument. Fear grips me anew, as if it were the first. Pavelek and I watch helplessly as my mother's lips tighten and her face gels into a mask. She disappears behind the mask. Only her pain remains.

It seeps into my belly. I want to run, to hide, just like we hide from the Germans. I pull a footstool up to the front door, climb up, and stretch my arm as far as it will go. My fingers barely reach the chain to slide it off. The bottom latch is easy.

Chapter 3

My parents, deep in their mutual trance, don't object. They know where to find me.

I slip out of the apartment, Pavelek snug in my arms. I scoot next door and, on tiptoes, strain to reach the doorbell. Janina welcomes me in.

"Hanka," she calls to her daughter, my little friend. "Irenka came to play with you."

If Janina knows the reason for my frequent visits, she doesn't let on. She offers me a cookie, but my stomach hurts too much to eat. Hanka chomps on hers, and then we play air raid. We hide Pavelek and Hanka's stuffed rabbit in a "bomb shelter" of overturned chairs.

My mother comes for me. I scan her face. She exists again. I skip home by her side.

But when the arguments explode at night, there is no place to hide.

CHAPTER FOUR

Father's Wet-Nurse

A rich child often sits
in a poor mother's lap.
—Spanish Proverb

Kasia was my father's wet-nurse. Although she had passed away by the time I was born, without her I would not have survived.

Kasia entered my father's life in the winter of 1903, just a week or two after his birth.

Like many Jews in the city of Przemysl, my grandparents, Jehudah and Gizela Licht, operated a small business. They owned two retail shops. One featured men's ready-to-wear clothing. The other—my father's favorite—fashioned ladies' hats, extravagantly decorated with beads, bows, feathers, and silk flowers. Since my grandfather spent long hours davening, or praying, in the synagogue, Grandma bustled back and forth between the two stores. Except for Shabbat dinner (schmaltz herring and gefilte fish, chicken soup, pot roast, and carrot tzimmes), she rarely returned from work before dark. With her first two children, she somehow managed. But when my father, little Szymek, arrived only two years after his brother, she decided to seek help. It was January and bitterly cold.

A peasant woman, reputed to be honest, had recently given birth in a nearby village. With my infant father wrapped in a shawl, Grandma climbed into a horse-drawn sleigh and rattled over snowy, rutted roads to check out this new mother, Kasia.

Kasia welcomed Grandma into her primitive farm shack. She was holding a baby to her breast and radiated peace and patience, despite a bevy of barefoot children pattering around on the cold floor. A skinny girl, maybe three, squatted by her side as she nursed the new baby. Kasia identified the little girl as her older daughter, Maria, nicknamed Marysia. The other youngsters were nieces and nephews. About fifteen people shared the tiny hut.

Kasia and her large family were clearly very poor. This was true of many Polish peasants, whose meager crops did not suffice to feed their children. To make ends meet, some hired themselves out as servants to the relatively well-to-do city dwellers, some of whom were Jews.

My grandmother offered to hire Kasia as a mamka, a wet-nurse. Kasia would live in my grandparents' home and nurse infant Szymek with the milk still flowing for her own baby. In addition, she would care for the two older children, cook, clean, wash clothes, and haul water from the well. In return, Grandma would provide room and board, plus a small salary. Kasia's children, of course, would have to remain behind on the farm.

Kasia stroked her infant's tiny cheek as she considered the offer. She got up to peek at the bundle in Grandma's arms.

"I have to discuss this with my sisters," she said, "and with Jesus."

She sliced off a piece of black bread from a half-eaten loaf lying on the scuffed kitchen table. She smeared it thickly with butter, scraped out of a practically empty tub, and set it on a wooden plate.

"Help yourself," she offered. "Please."

Then she disappeared, shutting the door gently behind her.

A flock of fluttering little fingers reached toward Grandma as soon as Kasia went out. Only Marysia remained quietly in her spot by Kasia's chair. Grandma distributed chunks of her bread until nothing remained. The children devoured it with guilty giggles.

Within an hour, Kasia had made up her mind. She appeared with a few possessions tied into a colorful scarf. A slightly older woman followed her in, holding Kasia's baby.

"My sister still has milk from this one," Kasia explained, pointing to a round-faced toddler on the floor. "She will nurse my Zosia, and take good care of Marysia, too."

As the two women climbed into the buggy, several

relatives materialized and waved. *Idz z Bogiem*, "Go with God," they shouted. Little Marysia crouched on the stoop, her head sunk in her lap.

•   •   •   •   •

My father's cradle, gaily painted with rabbits and roosters, was placed in the kitchen by Kasia's bed. She lavished on this little Jewish stranger the milk and the love meant for her own infant. And the two grew inseparable. As a little boy, Szymek would often climb in bed with her; she called him her little stove. Of the three siblings, Szymek would always be her favorite.

Kasia remained with the Licht family for more than twenty years. Each Monday she sent the few zlotys she earned to the relatives back home. It wasn't much, but it put food on their table. She kept almost nothing for herself.

Still, it was not enough. Zosia, my father's "milk sister," died of tuberculosis when she was just eleven years old. Marysia barely survived.

•   •   •   •   •

In Grandma's bright kitchen, a big pot of potatoes is bubbling on the stove. Kasia is making pierogi. Szymek, now a small boy of three or four, standing on a stool, eagerly awaits his chance to help. Kasia lets him punch the sticky dough after she has kneaded it with her strong hands. His fingers are covered with flour. He places them on the rolling pin right next to Kasia's. Together they roll out the dough, then carve out circles with a water glass.

My father, on the left, with Aunt Berta and Uncle Izek.

Now Kasia chops onions. Their sting sends Szymek scampering, but he runs right back to help mash the boiled potatoes until they are smooth as cream. Kasia fries the onions, stirs them into the potatoes, and adds a generous slab of goose fat, a pinch of salt. As Kasia supervises, the little boy carefully ladles spoonfuls of the mixture on the dough rounds. Kasia folds them in half and seals them into ears, or half-moons. Together they arrange the raw pierogi on a clean dishtowel while they wait for water to boil.

"Stay clear of the kettle, little Szymek," Kasia warns as she slides each ear into the steaming pot. In moments the pierogi rise to the top. The first one done, hot and bathed in butter, is set to cool on Szymek's special plate. He always gets the first.

•   •   •   •   •

When Szymek is about five, the circus comes to town. His big brother Izek, and Izek's friends, plan to sneak in.

Szymek overhears the scheme. To keep him from tattling, the boys reluctantly invite him to tag along. The older ones nimbly scale a sagging section of the fence around the circus grounds. The last to go, Szymek struggles to follow, but the fence is too high for him. The other boys disappear into the circus tent without a backward glance.

Szymek trudges home to Kasia in tears. He confesses. Instead of scolding, Kasia pulls a little satchel from under her pillow. A few coins spill out onto the kitchen table.

"Go buy yourself a ticket," she says, inviting him to pick out enough coins for the price of admission to the circus. Szymek counts the money. A ticket would cost all she had.

"I don't want to go," Szymek lies, and climbs into her lap.

Kasia's eyes are wet now, too.

"Those other boys might have the circus," she croons, hugging him, "but you, my little one, will always have Kasia."

"This was the magic word," my father later recalled. "I was happy. I didn't cry any more. I felt that I was rich, the other boys were poor: I was Kasia's."

•   •   •   •   •

Little Szymek and Kasia pore over his homework. Together they trace letters on a slate and sing out their sounds. He helps her along. Together they learn to read. Her face lights up when the meaningless squiggles in her little white Bible start to click into sacred words.

●   ●   ●   ●   ●

Like most Poles, Kasia was a devout Catholic.

"She never tried to convert me," my father said. "In fact, she always told all three of us: 'Go to the synagogue with your Papa. He needs his children by his side.'"

Kasia spent hours teaching my father's sister to strike matches safely, so that Berta could light the Shabbat candles; she guided the hands of the two boys on the knife as they learned to slice challah. Still, Szymek insisted that she take him with her to church on Sundays. By the time he was grown, he could recite by heart the entire Catholic mass as well as the major Jewish prayers. In his heart of hearts, he was as much Catholic as Jew.

●   ●   ●   ●   ●

During Kasia's many years with the Licht family, her two daughters often came to visit. They were close in age to my father and his siblings, and all five children played, squabbled and loved each other like brothers and sisters.

When Zosia, Kasia's younger daughter, died, Tatus and Marysia cried in each other's arms. The tragedy formed an even stronger bond between them. As they grew into adolescents, their friendship continued to deepen, perhaps even verging on a secret romance.

Because she loved him, Marysia never complained to my father. She never shared the pain she must have felt in having to give up her own mother to him. As fate would have it, one day my father would be giving his daughter to Marysia.

CHAPTER FIVE

Marysia: An Angel

It is most remarkable that those flowers which are
most emblematic of purity should grow in the mud.
—Henry David Thoreau

In the fall of 1941, the Nazi persecution of Jews got even
worse. All of Poland's Jews were ordered to move into
ghettos—areas especially established for them, to keep them
apart from non-Jews.

My parents realized that entering the ghetto could be
suicide, and so they looked for alternatives. There was a little
breathing space before the deadline to leave our home.
Exchanging diamonds for money, my parents obtained "false
papers." At that time, everyone in Poland had identification
papers, somewhat more detailed than American birth
certificates. Ours specifically identified us as Jews.

For a price, some Poles were willing to sell their papers—and my parents were lucky to have that price. My mother bought her papers from a woman named Pola Kaliszewska, my father from Mieczyslaw Teodorowicz. Mine belonged to a child two years older than myself. Her name was Teresa Chrystyna Urban—and that was who I would soon become.

Armed with these new identities, my parents made plans to leave Lvov. But they knew that they would not be able to escape with a child in tow. My father dashed off an urgent letter to Kasia's daughter.

"Marysia, we need you right away," he wrote. She arrived the next day. It was the first time I had ever seen her.

· · · · ·

This is how I remember the scene: as a motionless frieze. The four of us still and stiff like statues in the park. I am five. We are in the "hiding room" behind the china closet. My mother and I face each other. A scuffed brown suitcase splits the emptiness between us. Only our gazes touch. Behind my mother, shrouded in shadow, my father's form fades into a chair. And right behind me looms the stranger, Marysia.

It must have been different, in those final moments before Marysia took me away. There must have been hugs, kisses, words of . . . words of what? But in my mind only the memory of a motionless frieze remains.

Then, suddenly, Marysia lifts the suitcase and takes my hand. We hurry down three flights of stairs, down into the dark street. In these simple steps, my family has disappeared. I have disappeared, too. I'm no longer Irena Stefania Licht.

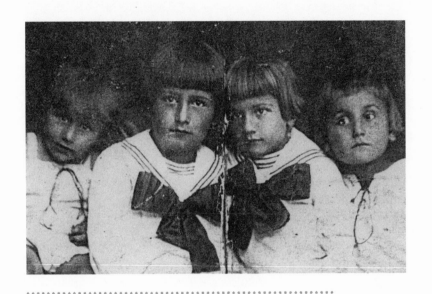

Marysias's four sons—a few years before my arrival.

I'm Teresa Chrystyna Urban, a girl two years older than myself. I like being older. I like my new name, too. Tereska. It sounds like *truskawka*—a strawberry. But it isn't really me. And Marysia is no longer a stranger; she is *Ciocia*, my "aunt."

Marysia carries the battered brown suitcase that my mother has packed. I suddenly realize that we have forgotten my doll Pavelek. It's too late to turn back. Marysia folds her free arm around my shoulders. Her rough black coat brushes my cheek. It smells of cold and mothballs. She strokes my arm through my old winter coat, worn and skimpy now, but still warm. She straightens my hat, the navy-blue one with a wide brim and ear flaps. My thick brown stockings itch. My shoes,

Chapter 5

laced to the ankles, pinch my toes. A fluffy muff hangs from my neck, suspended by a string. I hug the muff instead of Pavelek.

I want to wave to my parents, but Marysia does not allow me to linger. She shepherds me briskly through the dark streets toward the train station.

The station is empty in the night. Our footsteps echo, and we try to quiet them. A couple of drunks snore on the lone bench. We sit on the other side of the bench and wait for the train.

Marysia rehearses me: What is my name? Teresa Chrystyna Urban, Tereska for short. How old am I? Seven. What is my religion? Catholic. Where are my parents? Dead; I am an orphan. Who is Marysia? Marysia is my aunt. My mother was her sister. I am going to live with my aunt.

We repeat these facts until I get them right, quickly, with no hesitation. I work at remembering. Then I work at for-getting—forgetting that I am Jewish. That my name is Irena. That I am Jewish. That I am only five. That I am Jewish. That I have parents who have sent me away.

The train rumbles into the station. We climb on. I fall asleep on Marysia's lap. She covers me with her rough coat, to keep me warm—and to hide me.

The train rattles through most of the night, covering the sixty miles between Lvov and Przemysl. Dim stars still dot the sky when we arrive. I stumble, sleep-groggy, as Marysia guides me toward number 10 Tadeusz Kosciuszko Street. We stop at a two-story house that overlooks the river. I head for the front entrance, but Marysia redirects me to a rickety wooden staircase in the backyard. She hauls the suitcase. I follow, grasping a wobbly banister.

Marysia cautions me to make no noise. Later I learn that the bottom two floors are occupied by the Polish police. We trudge up to the third floor, which is actually the attic. This is Marysia's home.

●　●　●　●　●

"Let her cry." That's the next thing I remember. "Let her cry. It will make her feel better."

I had a dream. In it I am holding Pavelek, touching his smooth porcelain face. Then I turn him over—but instead of his hair, another face stares at me from the back of his head. My doll has turned into a monster. Jolted awake from the dream, I feel panicked. It takes me a while to orient myself, even to the fact that I am crying. I burrow deeper into my cave, under unfamiliar covers. My fingers search for Pavelek, who always sleeps with me, but find only a tangle of starched linens. Now my sobs, which I try to squelch, shake the whole bed.

"Let her cry," the voice repeats. A gentle voice. Marysia. There are other voices, lots of them, it seems to me. I cautiously peek out from under the covers and see many legs with pants on. Curiosity calms my sobs—curiosity and Marysia's quiet voice. I sit up.

The single room that makes up Marysia's living quarters throbs with activity. Four teenage boys are milling around in a space not much bigger than our shelter behind the china closet. I see two big beds, including the one in which I find myself, a table and three chairs, a wood stove, a cabinet with dishes, a dishpan, and a sewing machine. The machine whirrs as Marysia's foot pumps the pedal.

For the first time I really look at the woman who has whisked me away from my parents. She is slim, with salt-and-pepper hair smoothed back into a tight bun. An oval face, light skin, soft green eyes. She wears a plain black dress, topped with a dark gray sweater. I gaze with fascination at her fingers, which fly as she tugs at a piece of royal-blue cloth.

The delicious smell of potatoes sizzling in lard stokes my hunger. It blends with the pungent odor of wood smoke and the strange scent of male sweat. I am an only child; the smell of boys is new to me.

Two of the boys are slicing potatoes and frying them on the woodstove. Two others are roughhousing. But all the action stops when my head pops out from under the covers. The boys line up on the bed across the room. They stare at me with a curiosity equal to mine. Marysia stops pedaling, and the sewing machine stops whirring. She smiles at me.

"This is your new sister, Tereska," she tells her sons. "We are all going to take good care of her."

She introduces the clan on the opposite bed:

Staszek. Seventeen. The man of the house, now that Marysia's husband has been sent to serve with the German forces in Hungary. Staszek's eyes are dark. He is tall, with powerful arms. He doesn't smile.

Zbyszek. Fifteen. A rather thrown-together boy, shirttails hanging out, hair messy, hands rough and dirty. He grins broadly and winks at me. Zbyszek helps Staszek with the

My "brothers" Zbyszek and Jurek.

chores, Marysia explains. They must chop wood in the forest and haul water from a distant well. Sometimes the boys sell wood to make money for food.

Jurek. Thirteen. He looks different from his brothers. While they are dark, with rough, angular features, Jurek's complexion is light, his face rounded, his eyes a soft green. He resembles his mother. Marysia addresses Jurek: "Your special job will be to take care of Tereska. You must always watch her, never leave her alone. You know how dangerous it is now, for all of us." Jurek beams a mischievous, crooked little grin that crinkles one of his cheeks more than the other.

Janek. Eleven. A small, thin boy, the baby of the family. Janek gazes shyly at the floor as his mother explains how much he helps in church and how well he sings in the choir.

Chapter 5

Our attic in Przemysl.

As if on cue, all four boys break into song, harmonizing lustily and making gestures to indicate that this is a "welcome song" for me. We all break out laughing when they finish. Marysia fixes me a plate of fried potato slices and a piece of black bread sprinkled with sugar.

●　●　●　●　●

I lived with Marysia and her family for two years.

Somewhere in that time, the boys' father, Jozef, returned. He was a swarthy man with a sizable mustache. He worked as a carpenter in a factory and spent his free time playing the harmonica and drinking vodka with his buddies. On payday, Staszek, the eldest son, often met him at the factory—to intercept some of his wages before they got drowned in the tavern. Jozef would part with only a fraction of the money. Later, when he came home, he would snore loudly on the bed. Occasionally he would get angry and thrash his sons for some transgression. He would order them to pull down their pants and I would watch in fear and fascination as one boy or another darted around the room, bare-bottomed, the father chasing with a belt and Marysia trying to step in between them.

Fights sometimes erupted between the boys. I recall Staszek shoving little Janek down the wobbly back staircase, punching him in the nose, blood gushing. Strangely enough, this open violence did not disturb me as much as had the verbal battles between my parents. There was something cleaner about it: a storm that blew over and passed, leaving no muggy residue.

● ● ● ● ●

No one but Marysia knew where my parents had gone. She kept the secret from me, from her children, from her husband. When I cried, missing them, she would tell me that they were well and that they loved me. To me, it seemed they had totally vanished.

I did have relatives nearby. My four-year-old cousin Olek was in hiding with another Christian woman in Przemysl. He was the only child of my father's brother Izek. Marysia had

Marysia and me in 1943.

arranged this placement for him, since she could not keep both of us in her home. Olek, like myself, had false papers and a different name. Marysia told me that Olek cried and fussed a lot, that he couldn't understand why his parents had left him. She worried about him and commended me for not showing such feelings. But she understood the bouts of loneliness that sometimes sent me under the bedcovers in the middle of the day. And she did everything she could to cheer me up.

One afternoon when I was particularly mopey, Marysia proposed a special treat: a visit to my beloved Aunt Berta. Much to my surprise, it turned out that Aunt Berta and her family were still living in Przemysl. They had complied with the Nazis' order to move into the Jewish ghetto. Most non-Jews who were not on official Nazi business kept far away from the ghetto. Both within and outside the barbed-wire fence enclosing this area, the sounds of gunshots and screams were frequently heard. The Jews were never let out. But outsiders, non-Jews, were allowed to visit if they wished.

Marysia offered to take me there. Knowing nothing of the ghetto, I was absolutely thrilled with the plan.

●　●　●　●　●

The ghetto is quiet this afternoon. No one bothers us as Marysia, my hand in hers, searches for Aunt Berta's address. My aunt greets us joyfully, with laughter and tears. In her extremely cramped quarters, with practically nothing to eat, she somehow manages to whip up a feast. I play and cuddle with my two cousins, who treat me like a precious toy.

The hours whiz by. Dusk descends. It's time to leave; we must not remain beyond the curfew hour. I am showered with kisses. My aunt presses me to her bosom and wipes her tears as we say goodbye.

The ghetto's streets are empty in the evening haze. Marysia and I, still glowing from our visit, stroll leisurely toward the gate. A German sentry passes us by and then, suddenly, turns back. Halt! He motions us with his rifle to a guards' hut nearby. There, in a quiet, polite tone of voice, he converses with Marysia, who speaks German. I understand nothing of what they say, but I know that something is wrong.

With no warning, the guard lowers his eyes to meet mine.

"Is this your mother?" he asks in broken Polish.

Marysia is supposed to be my aunt. Has she told the guard that she is my mother? I glance at his gun and make a quick decision.

"Yes," I say. I hold my breath. He lets us go.

That one word, "yes," saved our lives that day.

●　●　●　●　●

Over time, the memories of my parents faded, like old photographs. The game of make-believe turned into reality; I grew into my part. The attic at 10 Tadeusz Kosciuszko Street became home, and Marysia's four boys my brothers. It no longer seemed strange to call Marysia "Aunt." At times, by mistake, I called her Mama.

If my brothers were jealous, they didn't let on. The only hint of resentment lay, perhaps, in rather merciless tickling sessions, during which I had to beg them to stop. But most of the time, under Marysia's strict instructions, the boys protected me. They carried me on their shoulders up the hill to the castle. They taught me how to play ducks, or what we call skippingstones, in the River San. They guarded me whenever we ventured outdoors, when anyone might ask: "Is this really your mother's niece?"

My brothers had to perform the most ignoble of tasks. The attic had no plumbing. To get to the outhouse, one had to trek down the three flights of stairs, passing the windows of the Polish police officers who lived on the floors below. In order to minimize contact with them, I was spared trips to the outhouse. Marysia installed a potty for me in the crawlspace above the attic, and the boys took turns emptying it out.

Like Kasia before her, Marysia respected everyone's religious beliefs. She did not try to convert me. She was, however, deeply devout, and she took her "niece" to Sunday mass, at the Catholic church.

* * * * *

I hold her hand as we enter the church lobby. Marysia dips her fingers in a bowl of holy water. She crosses herself. I hear singing. We walk through heavy carved doors into the sanctuary. The scent of incense floats out to greet us. The church is crowded. Marysia kneels and crosses herself again. We slide into a wooden pew. I look around, notice my brother Janek in a long red and white gown. He is an altar boy. The priest mounts the steps of a balcony. His voice rises to a roar as he warns his flock to do right and shun sin. I tremble and squeeze Marysia's hand.

The next times we go to church, I am less afraid. I learn to love the beautiful artwork, the incense, the songs, the prayers. I envy the people partaking in communion, their serene faces and folded hands as they return from the altar to their pews. Mostly I love the statue of the Virgin Mary gazing at Baby Jesus with soft eyes. I pretend that baby is me.

●　●　●　●　●

Time passed. Danger surrounded us, not only from the Germans, but also from the Polish and Ukrainian police. Harboring Jews was strictly forbidden. Several Poles in Przemysl were shot for this crime.

Yet in the midst of my loving family, I felt secure. There are times, even today, when I need to crawl into a space that is safe. At those times, I close my eyes and travel back to Marysia's dimly lit attic. I see her bending over the sewing machine, feeding fabric under the needle. The machine rumbles softly, like a satisfied baby. I slip into the chair by her side. We do not speak. She calmly goes on with her work. And her aura envelops me in peace. I feel loved. Her love flows freely, naturally, as sweet as mother's milk.

With Marysia by my side, I said prayers at bedtime, continued to go to church, and listened to my brothers sing in the choir. They sang at home, too, sometimes accompanied by Staszek, the oldest, on a scratchy violin, and sometimes by their father on his sprightly harmonica. The attic shook with their lusty voices; we worried that the police downstairs would complain.

They sang Christmas carols, *koledy*, the beautiful, soulful melodies that gave me goosebumps. At Christmastime it seemed that the whole shabby attic radiated warmth. The boys would chop down a pine tree and burst in with much fanfare, song, and the fresh fragrance of the forest. We would all sit on the floor cutting out and pasting together paper chains and angels. And late on Christmas Eve, how exciting it was to be woken and bundled up for the trudge through the crispy snow to midnight mass.

For the first year and a half of my life with Marysia's family, I rarely left the attic apartment. Marysia and her husband worried that someone might become suspicious about the little girl whom they called her niece. After the close call in the ghetto, Marysia became even more cautious. But the months rolled by without any further incident. On the few occasions when my brothers did take me out—to the castle in the park, perhaps, or down to the river to play skipping-stones—nobody bothered us. And so Marysia became bolder: She enrolled me in preschool. I was six, maybe seven, by then. All went well for several months. But then my school career came to an abrupt end.

• • • • •

We are rehearsing a play for Mother's Day. I have memorized the song that we will sing:

Chapter 5

Let us all say thank you
To our loving mother
Who always cares about us,
Always cares about us
Though we are a bother

This is to be my first stage appearance, and I can hardly wait. The fact of my own mother's absence does not disturb me; Marysia will be there.

Marysia comes, but not in the manner I have expected. In the middle of the rehearsal, the director of the school walks into the classroom, whispers to the teacher, and escorts me out into the hall. There stands Marysia, my beat-up brown suitcase by her side, a stuffed shopping bag hanging from her arm.

We head straight for the railroad station. Without going home. Without saying goodbye.

We have to escape from Przemysl: My little cousin Olek has been captured by the Nazis.

Poor Olek had not been able to adjust to his new life and identity. On this particular day he had been playing on the street with some children. A fight broke out, as the children teased him about not having parents. In a fit of anger, Olek shouted: "I do, too, have parents. And my real name is Olek Licht, and I come from Lvov. I want to go home!"

The children ran to report the news to their elders, who then informed the Polish police. The Gestapo rushed in and dragged Olek away. They soon found his parents, who were hiding elsewhere. We wondered at the coincidence. Had someone in Przemysl denounced them? The woman with whom he had been staying, perhaps? No harm came to her. Did she trade her life for theirs? We never saw Olek or his parents again. The Nazis must have murdered them all.

With Olek caught, Marysia believed that it was only a matter of time before the Nazis would be looking for me as well. News traveled fast in Przemysl. People knew that two strange children had arrived in town within days of each other. One had turned out to be Jewish. Could the other one be Jewish, too? We could not take the chance. We had to run.

Marysia did not explain all this to me at the time. She did not want to frighten me. All she said was, "We are going on a trip," and she rushed me straight from school to the train station.

"Where are we going?" I asked.

"I can't tell you right now. I'll tell you when we get there."

We boarded a train to Warsaw.

Not knowing what else to do, Marysia headed for my parents. She alone knew their address. When she left her house that day, she left no message for her family—the less they knew, the better. There might be interrogations.

And there were. Every day, I later learned, the Germans interrogated Marysia's husband, Jozef. Her sons Staszek and Jurek were deported to labor camps in Germany. Zbyszek and Janek escaped to hide with an aunt on a farm. It was months before Marysia dared to contact Jozef, months before she knew whether her husband and children were even alive.

My parents were in hiding in Warsaw. A friend had referred them to an elderly Russian countess, Lady Valentina

Mlodecka, who lived alone and suffered from many real and imagined illnesses. She had agreed to hide my parents in her apartment. In exchange, my father would be constantly available to provide her with medical care and emotional support.

It was only as our train approached the Warsaw station that Marysia told me we were going to see my parents. It would be a surprise, since she had not had time to inform them. I was, of course, thrilled at the prospect.

We entered a building, climbed a flight of stairs, and Marysia rang the bell at number 1B. Waiting for the door to open, I could hardly breathe. I pictured my parents' joyful faces when they saw me. The door opened. My father froze. His face telegraphed terror.

It was not the welcome I had imagined. "Daddy has a mustache," I ventured, instead of jumping into his arms. He hustled us inside. My mother's reaction made up somewhat for my father's. She just hugged me and hugged me and laughed and wept all at the same time. "I thought I would never see you again," she kept crying, as she held me in her arms. "I thought I would never see you again."

I was glad to see her. But I didn't cry. Much as I had been excited at the prospect of reuniting with my parents, they now seemed like strangers to me. It had been two years. More than a quarter of my life. When they went to discuss my arrival with the Countess, I was glad to cuddle up next to Marysia.

* * * * *

"We have a child, Lady Vala," my parents told the Countess. "We were afraid to tell you."

"She cannot stay here," the Countess said. "I'm sorry. Our tenant will not fail to notice."

A German officer lived in another one of the rooms in Lady Vala's apartment. He did not pay rent, of course, but occasionally he gave the Countess food coupons to be exchanged for goods at the special German supply store. His presence terrified my parents, and they carefully stayed out of his way. When they did cross paths, he gave no indication of suspecting that they were Jewish. But a child—especially one with olive skin and dark, curly hair like me—would arouse his curiosity.

I had to leave.

CHAPTER SIX

. . . .

The Convent

Where does God dwell?
God dwells wherever man lets him in.
   —The Kotzk Rebbe, 1787–1859

On cloudy days in Warsaw, the flat gray walls of the convent were barely distinguishable from the gloom of the sky. The building's stark facade faded in the haze. For those wishing to enter, a broad stairway led to heavy double doors, which, in contrast to the barren surroundings, were ornamented with intricate religious motifs. A sign above the doors read: Home for Orphans and Poor Children. Marysia and I knocked.

Inside, a dim vestibule opened onto long corridors that stretched like tunnels to either side. Echoes bounced between the stone floors and high ceilings. A solitary nun glided slowly by, submerged in a tent of black robes. More sisters followed, all alike, their fingers nimbly counting rosaries, their small faces pinched by austere, stiff white frames.

An acrid odor of kerosene saturated the air. Except, perhaps, in the chapel, where it was masked by the intoxicating fragrance of incense and, on special occasions, rose petals. The chapel boasted a stained-glass window and a finely chiseled statue of the Virgin Mother, who gazed with eternal tenderness upon her infant son.

The other children who lived in the convent had no mothers. They ran around in the back rooms, clad in thin, shabby dresses and thick, patched stockings. Some sat in corners, their eyes fixed on their own invisible worlds.

The stench of kerosene grew stronger on the way to the washrooms. Entering this area, one passed a series of toilet seats, stacked up against a white tiled wall. There were no doors or partitions, just toilets, usually topped with small bare bottoms. Beyond was a large room with deep sinks. A beehive of activity buzzed here. Aproned nuns energetically scrubbed kerosene into children's lice-infested heads. Other nuns carefully inspected the scalps of formerly disinfected subjects. Those who passed were sent away with squeals of delight. Those whose hair still glistened with shiny white nits had to submit to a razor-wielding nun. Soon they emerged tearful and bald.

Not far from the washroom stood the dining hall. Here the kerosene fumes mingled with a smell resembling stagnant dishwater. Occasionally, when the door to the nuns' dining

Children rescued by Franciscan sisters in another Warsaw convent.

room had been left open, an inviting aroma of real chicken soup would waft in.

The children ate diluted potato stew, ladled from an enormous pail into eighty small bowls. The recipients carried this fare to long tables, where the hungry ones surreptitiously acquired seconds from those who had long ago lost their appetites. The stew was accompanied by gritty black bread, whose taste could be somewhat improved by squeezing it until a sticky, clay-like consistency was achieved.

There were bedrooms of a sort, dormitories where numerous beds stood in rows like desks in a schoolroom.

Most evenings the youngsters obediently went to sleep after saying their prayers and folding their arms across their chests, as instructed by the nuns. But some nights a ghost would stir the mattress of one child or another, and a panicky exodus into the darkened corridors would ensue. And when the full moon shone boldly through the naked windowpanes, certain children, referred to as "lunatics," might wander up the walls in total defiance of gravity.

Then there were nights when screaming sirens ripped through the thick gray walls. On those nights, nuns and children would leave their beds and file silently down to the bomb shelter. They huddled close together around a single small candle whose flicker threw weak shadows across the sweating cellar pipes. A musty underground dampness pervaded the atmosphere. One nun, her black robes melted by the darkness, rose to lead them all in song to God. Their voices resounded through the shelter, almost drowning out the thunder of falling bombs.

• • • • •

The Mother Superior eyes me critically the day Marysia brings me to register at the orphanage.

"The child is dark," she says, pointing to the brown curls that escape from the long braids hanging down to my hips. "Could be taken for a Gypsy."

A code word for Jew.

"You should not take her out too much," she advises.

Maybe my parents stole me from the Gypsies, I think. I'm not really their child. No wonder they keep sending me away.

The Mother Superior glides out from behind her desk. She puts a hand on my shoulder.

"Say goodbye to your aunt now. I'll show you to the children's rooms."

Somehow it hadn't occurred to me that Marysia would leave me here, that she would go away. But now Marysia is putting on her coat, bending down for a parting hug.

"I'll visit you soon," she promises, and before I can lock my arms around her neck, she is gone.

● ● ● ● ●

Two and a half years in the orphanage. For the first few months, I didn't utter a single word. I no longer knew who I was supposed to be, what I was supposed to say, and what secrets I was supposed to keep. I stumbled around my dormitory, a silent shadow. The nuns ignored me, reserving their ministrations for more rambunctious children. Actually, the adults were absent most of the time. One of the older orphans, a teenage girl, meted out discipline. She checked nightly under our blankets to make sure that our hands were folded in prayer position or crossed demurely across our chests—never below the waist. She smacked children with a wooden paddle for fighting or laughing or crying, or for no reason at all.

I generally escaped her notice. I followed rules, learned lengthy prayers, and peeled potatoes.

The potatoes were served in a stew with some sort of gravy. It made me nauseous. I refused to eat at all. This eventually attracted attention. Worried about my health, the nuns invited me for a meal in their own dining room. I gobbled up a delicious soup—real chicken and cabbage. The sisters felt reassured that this one good meal would ensure my survival. They returned me to the children's cafeteria and the inedible slop dished out there.

Marysia came to visit every few weeks. She brought a paper bag of sweets sent by my parents. Of course I could not admit to having parents, so they never visited themselves. Every month or so, though, Marysia would sneak me into Lady Vala's apartment to see them. Marysia lived with them there now.

My parents tried to make these rare visits into special events. Even the Countess joined in, sharing her German food coupons. Either Marysia or my father would run to the German store to trade them in for white bread, perhaps, or a few slices of ham. My father sometimes risked exposure by taking me for brief outdoor excursions. He trusted his "non-incriminating" appearance. With his fair skin, light gray eyes, and straight, light brown hair, he could blend in with the general Polish population. My mother, on the other hand, looked Jewish. Despite her bleached-blonde hair, she had an olive complexion and dark eyes that made it harder for her to "pass" for Christian.

●　　●　　●　　●　　●

One snowy morning in 1944, my father takes me sledding. He bundles me up and we follow the ring of children's laughter to a long, gentle hill nearby. Sleds fly by as we explore the slope. We don't own a sled, but this does not discourage my father. He approaches a girl of twelve or so who seems to be sledding alone, and introduces me.

"This is Tereska," he tells her. "She is an orphan. Would you give her a ride on your sled?"

The girl eyes him dubiously.

"Jesus blesses children who help orphans, you know," my father says.

This works. The girl scoots to the front of the sled, and I hop on behind her. We zoom down the snowy hill, trudge back up, slide down again and again. The cold spray of snowflakes stings our cheeks and makes them rosy. The girl shows me how to steer, and we switch seats. A sense of power surges through me as the sled swerves at my command. We both screech with laughter whenever it flips us into the snow.

"It's time to go back now," my father says, after what seems like a brief moment. "They will be waiting with lunch."

I reluctantly brush myself off.

"Can you come again tomorrow?" the girl asks.

I look at my father.

"Maybe not tomorrow," he says. "Another day."

But I know that the snow will have melted by the time I visit my parents again.

With my fun interrupted, I feel grumpy and eager for the comfort of my mother's arms. We don't expect Marysia to return before evening; she works at a dressmaker's shop. But when we get home, my mother is gone, too.

"Where is Pola?" my father asks the Countess, using my

Marysia visits me and my friend Koziol at the convent, in 1943.

mother's current fake name. He sounds frightened.

"Don't worry," she reassures him. "You weren't here, so I asked her to run over to the German store. Herr Schmidt gave me coupons for white bread, and I know how Tereska loves it."

"She shouldn't have gone out," my father says. His voice sounds strained, but I know that he won't let the Countess see the full extent of his anger.

"It's only one block from here," Lady Vala says. "And besides, she has the German coupons. Who would bother her?"

"When did she leave?" my father asks.

"Half an hour ago, maybe. Sometimes there's a long line. She should be back in a few minutes."

We wait. The Countess gets out of bed and puts on her silk aqua robe. Together we set the table for lunch, carefully arranging translucent china plates and sparkling crystal glasses—very different tableware from that used at the convent! The minutes pass—and then an hour. My father is pacing up and down. Lady Vala urges us to start eating. She is sure there is just a long line at the store. After all, it's Saturday. People are shopping for the big meal on Sunday. But my father is not hungry and neither am I. The Countess returns to bed. The plates on the table remain empty. A dense fog seems to settle on us all. My father stares out the window, his face ashen, his lips moving silently. Lady Vala swallows a pill, closes her eyes.

I watch the hands of the pendulum clock. The minute hand travels a full circle. My mother does not return. I think of the first morning that I woke up at Marysia's. I remember the nightmare of the two-faced Pavelek. I remember searching for my doll under the unfamiliar bedcovers, and the empty terror when nothing was there.

A key turns in the lock. The Countess struggles to sit up. My father and I dart toward the door. The door opens: It's Marysia, back from her job. For once, I am disappointed to see her. My father shrinks into himself.

"What is it?" Marysia asks.

He tells her.

Marysia verbalizes the thought that none of us has dared to speak: "They must have caught her."

She takes me in her arms, and I am finally able to cry. Nobody tries to reassure me. My father, who normally takes charge, now appeals to Marysia.

"What should we do?" he asks, and the childlike whimper in his voice scares me as much as my mother's absence.

"You should hide at the Bakowskis' for a while," Marysia says, accepting leadership. The Bakowskis are old patients of my father's and have helped my parents in the past. "You know the Gestapo will come here looking for you next. Meanwhile, I will take Tereska back to the convent."

The memory of the frantic flight from Przemysl flashes before my eyes. We were running from the Nazis then. This scenario I was familiar with. But what happens when they catch you? What will they do to my mother? I don't know, and I don't ask. I don't really want to know.

With a sigh indicating the force of great effort, my father gathers his resources.

"She will come back," he says. "God will bring her back."

He manages a weak smile, but I can tell he doesn't mean it.

"Let's pray," Marysia says.

The Countess struggles to get out of bed, and moves to a chair. Marysia helps her. Marysia and I kneel. My father stands behind the Countess, and we all join in as Marysia offers prayers to Jesus and to St. Jude, the patron saint of desperate causes.

That night, at the convent, dreams of Pavelek haunt me. He appears and disappears. I look in the doll carriage, but it's empty. In a half-awake state, I feel a ghost under my bed. I shiver in fear, but don't call anyone. Slowly the ghost disappears. In the morning I eat nothing at all and must look sick, because a nun sends me to the infirmary. They put a big thermometer under my armpit. My temperature is normal.

In the chapel for Sunday mass, I plead, "Dear Jesus, I'll never be naughty again. Please bring my mother back."

* * * * *

"Aren't you lucky," the sister in the lobby says that afternoon. "Your aunt is here for the second day in a row!"

Marysia is smiling. "I have good news!" she explodes, unable even to wait until we go outside. She signs me out. I'm allowed only a few minutes with her, since I was out yesterday. On the street, she tells me, "Your mother is home."

That's all she says, and it is enough. Mama is safe. Jesus and St. Jude answered our prayers.

• • • • •

It took months before my mother was ready to tell me what had happened on that awful day. While waiting to cash in her food coupons, a Pole of German origin—a Volksdeutscher— tapped her on the shoulder. These people were known for their virulent anti-Semitism, their hatred of Jews.

"You are Jewish," he said to my mother. "Come with me to Gestapo headquarters."

Mama protested that she was not Jewish and started to pull out her documents to prove it, but he insisted that he was right. She had no choice but to go with him.

The admissions officer at the Gestapo believed my mother. In fact, he scolded the informer.

"I wish that you would stop bringing in all these Poles for me to interrogate," he told him. "Most of them are Catholics. This woman does not look Jewish to me."

But the Volksdeutscher was adamant: My mother looked Jewish to him. He finally convinced the admissions officer, who then led my mother to a basement cell occupied by several other prisoners. They were awaiting interrogation for a variety of transgressions.

One prisoner offered advice: "I don't know if you are Jewish or not, but if you are, don't ever admit it," he told her. "No matter how hard they beat you and torture you."

She spent the night in the dark cell, preparing herself to die. She wasn't afraid of death, she told me.

"I worried most about you," she said. "Who would take care of you after they killed me?"

But they didn't kill her. Equipped with all the proper false papers, able repeatedly to recite her assumed family history, and fluent in Catholic prayers, she managed to convince the interrogator of her innocence. He judged her not guilty of the crime of being Jewish.

• • • • •

The relief over my mother's safety seemed to free me. I began to speak and to participate more fully in convent life.

The other children joined forces to save my hair. They sat with me for hours, pulling out nits. A girl named Koziol, meaning "goat," befriended me. She was a rough, noisy girl and enticed me into rumbles from which I emerged scratched and bruised. The teenager in charge hit us both with the paddle. I noticed that, for the first time, I could cry soundlessly; I was growing up.

CHAPTER SEVEN

First Communion

> . . . whatever I call myself
> I look the same
> I feel the same
> I cry
> and
> sing the same.
> —Rodolfo "Corky" Gonzales

I was eight years old, but my false papers said I was ten. This being the case, at the convent I was due for First Communion. I had seen the group before me, marching in the chapel, clad in delicate white dresses, with flowers in their hair. I had seen their lovely white Bibles, given to them by the Mother Superior, and the medallions of the Virgin Mary, which they wore on silver chains. I could hardly wait for my turn.

The next time Marysia visited, she took me for a walk.

"I have something very important to discuss with you," she said. "You are not a Catholic. It would be a sin for you to take communion."

"You mean I can't do First Communion?" I was heartbroken.

"It's even more serious than that. If we refuse to have you participate, the convent will know why. I think the Mother Superior suspects anyway, but the other sisters don't. We will have to withdraw you from the convent . . . unless . . ."

"Unless what?"

"Unless you would like to be baptized. I know a priest who is willing to do it. But it must be of your own free will. Otherwise, don't worry, we will find someplace else for you to go."

I weighed the choices: to be baptized and enjoy the coming festivities, or to leave the convent. I recalled my father's terror-stricken face when Marysia and I had appeared on his doorstep in Warsaw. If I left the convent, my parents would be terrified again. And goodness knows where they would send me next.

It was no contest.

"I want to be baptized," I said.

• • • • •

Under cover of darkness Marysia, my father, and I join the priest in an empty church. Out in the vestibule he murmurs prayers and sprinkles holy water on my head. I am a Catholic.

• • • • •

Now that I was a Catholic, I could celebrate First Communion. There were about a dozen of us candidates, all girls who had recently reached age ten. Because I was actually only eight, and quite small even for my real age, the other girls towered over me. The nuns in charge of preparing communion outfits clucked and shook their heads as they slipped one of the gauzy white gowns over my head. Some of the other dresses would need nipping and tucking, but mine required major surgery. It totally engulfed me.

The nuns attributed my dwarfed stature to "poor appetite" and began keeping a sharper eye on me in the cafeteria. It became more and more difficult for me to dump a half-eaten dish of turnips in the trash or on a neighbor's plate. They worried about me, I guess, but not enough to invite me to eat with them again.

Besides fittings for dresses, First Communion preparations involved intensive religious instruction. The hours devoted to lessons jumped from one a day to as many as four. We still had to attend regular school, but we were occasionally excused from chores, much to the envy of the younger orphans. For these special lessons, we were allowed into the chapel. We filed in on the plush carpet that ran down the center aisle. During the day, as the sun moved across the sky, the color of the carpet deepened from pale pink to fiery red. The sun worked even more magic on the two stained-glass windows that flanked the altar. Haloed saints glowed in the velvet colors of fresh pansies. The intoxicating smell of incense, always renewed during Sunday mass, lingered through the week.

Mother Superior herself taught the First Communion classes. The children were duly impressed and most of the time offered the rapt attention she demanded. She rarely had to use the ruler that was always handy by her side. Mother Superior was an elderly, heavy-set woman whose broad hips inflated her habit into a black balloon. I remembered her from my first day at the convent, when she warned Marysia that I looked like, well, like a Gypsy.

Much of the information that she gave us was familiar, but Mother Superior stressed it with extra fervor. In contrast to the usual silence maintained by the nuns, Mother Superior's voice rang throughout the chapel. It was because she loved us that she wanted us to really get the message, she said.

"You must understand what I'm telling you," she boomed, "because the life of your immortal soul is at stake."

Above all, she said, we must realize that we were sinners. As such, we were in constant danger of burning in hell for eternity.

"Can any of you imagine eternity?" she asked.

Nobody could, although it did seem like a very long time.

Bad children, of course, were at greatest risk, she explained. But even the well behaved among us had no guarantee of reaching heaven. We could easily find ourselves sucked into purgatory, that middle zone between heaven and hell, waiting and waiting for admission to a heaven that teased us just beyond our reach.

Hell did not faze me much. I never really feared it, despite having heard vivid descriptions of giant flames, stoked by devils with their pitchforks. Frankly, I didn't think I was bad enough to be sent there, especially now that I was a Catholic.

Purgatory, on the other hand, terrified me. I pictured it as the dark corner to which my mother used to exile me as a punishment. She would make me face the wall and wait endlessly for a reprieve. While tears ran down my face, I would hear the rest of the family going about its regular business. All the sounds in the apartment seemed to rise to thunderous levels: footsteps, dishes clattering, floorboards creaking, the icebox dripping, toilet flushing. Voices seemed magnified, but at the same time muffled, so that I would hear my mother shouting garbled nonsense to Babcia.

Worst were the times when my friend Hanka came to play. In the course of fooling around, I might break or spill something and my mother would send me to the corner, where I would cringe in shame as Hanka witnessed my humiliation.

One time Mama entirely forgot that she had sent me to the corner. Hanka got tired of waiting and went back to her apartment next door. The chain jingled in the latch as she let herself out. A lifetime—or perhaps an eternity—crawled by before my mother remembered me. Her hugs and apologies did little to ease the pain of being abandoned in a dark corner, facing the wall—and waiting. No, I wanted no part of purgatory.

Fortunately, there was a chance of avoiding both hell and purgatory. Jesus Christ, our Savior, created an opportunity

Children celebrating First Communion in Warsaw.

through the sacrament of communion. The Mother Superior paused to allow this remark to sink in. We, the candidates for First Communion, stood at the threshold of that opportunity.

"Jesus Christ came to earth just to open the gates to heaven," Mother Superior intoned. "He had to suffer agonies, because some evil people hated him."

She pointed to a large painting of Jesus on the cross.

Poor Jesus, I thought, as I always did when confronted with an image of the blood dripping from his wounds. I glanced at my favorite statue, the one of Baby Jesus in his mother's arms. Some monsters had nailed this baby to the cross. I hated them. Just like I hated the monsters who had snatched away my little cousin Olek.

"The evil ones were called Jews," Mother Superior declared.

She may as well have hit me with a hammer. Marysia had carefully shielded me from this aspect of Catholic belief. I had never heard it before. I wanted to scream: No, the Jews could not have killed Jesus. The Jews are good people, like my parents, and Aunt Berta and Olek and me.

Suddenly I remembered that little Olek had been arrested because he had revealed that he was a Jew. Did they think that he had killed Jesus? Olek . . . Jews . . . Jesus . . . . Previously unrelated fragments were beginning to form patterns like bits of glass in a kaleidoscope. I wanted to scream, but of course I knew better. I was well trained in the lessons of silence.

And besides, I caught myself thinking somewhat guiltily, it's got nothing to do with me. I'm a Catholic now.

• • • • •

The First Communion celebration fully lived up to its promise. But confession, required before taking communion, was hard. I had stayed up late into the night considering what sin I could report that would be worth the priest's time. Nothing came to mind until I recalled dumping my dinner plate into the trash bin behind the monitor's back. I wasn't sure that this would qualify, but the priest seemed satisfied. As I knelt in the privacy of the confession booth, he granted me absolution and assigned a certain number of Hail Marys to be prayed using the brand-new rosary beads that we had been given.

Now we were ready for the big event.

As the shortest in the group, I lead the procession of First Communicants to the altar. Spring flowers, lilacs and lilies-of- the-valley, decorate the altar and emit a heady fragrance, blending with the incense.

I feel as beautiful as a flower myself. My ankle-length white gown, altered by the nuns, hugs me perfectly at the waist, where it is tied with a satin bow. A daisy wreath crowns my hair and I carry a basket of rose petals, which I scatter along the sides of the aisle. The audience of children and nuns accompanies us with a harmony of hymns.

We kneel at the altar before the priest. He dips his fingers into a silver bowl and draws out a thin round wafer. He places it gently on my tongue.

"Don't bite!" I warn myself, picturing the wafer as the very body of Christ. I notice that it has no special taste. It feels in my mouth just like the wafer we shared in Marysia's family at Christmastime. But that one could be touched with one's teeth. I cradle the communion wafer carefully between my tongue and the roof of my mouth. Still kneeling at the altar as the other children receive their communion, I observe how the wafer softens and slowly dissolves. And as it dissolves, so do all my fears and sadness. And my body merges with the body of Christ. As I return to my pew with folded hands, I feel as clean and new as the air after a summer rain. Clean enough to ascend to heaven.

• • • • •

The path to heaven, however, turned out to be more bumpy than one would expect. According to Sister Frances, our next religious instructor, to get there you would have to die within seconds of receiving communion—that is how long a grace period most of us have before sinning again. At first this idea seemed preposterous. But after keeping track of my sins for the next few confessions, I realized that a few seconds was a generous estimate; it took hardly any time at all for me to snap at someone, tell a lie, think angry thoughts. All these, and many others, proved to be true transgressions, ones that could immediately disqualify me from heaven.

Heaven, in my mind, was a quiet little room, somewhat like Marysia's attic. In it, the Blessed Virgin sat rocking her holy infant. No bombs fell there to frighten away her peaceful smile. The hope of someday getting there helped to stem my panic during air raids. While waiting for the all-clear signal, I would plan how I could time my death to coincide with the moment of receiving communion. It did not seem like a promising prospect.

Fortunately, according to Sister Frances, there was another route to heaven.

"It won't be as easy as it sounds," she warned us. Nonetheless, we all leaned forward in our seats. I was not alone in my desire for salvation. "You have to attend confession and communion every week for nine months. No skipping. If you miss a single Sunday, you must start all over again."

Several hands flew up in the air. "Really?" "Honestly?" "Then you definitely will go to heaven?"

"Yes," Sister Frances assured us. "Only, like I said, it won't be easy."

Sounds easy to me, I thought. The nuns marched us to mass each Sunday anyway.

The first few weeks slipped by without a problem. I took communion regularly, always luxuriating in the radiant sense of sparkling purity.

Whereas all my peers set out to achieve perfect attendance, most dropped out within a few weeks. Illness grounded many. I resolved to keep sore throats, upset stomachs, and headaches to myself. Nevertheless, after six weeks or so, a high fever landed me in the infirmary. I missed mass two Sundays in a row. Disappointed, but undaunted, I resumed my count from scratch, keeping tabs on the remains of a paper bag in which Marysia had brought sourballs.

When three out of the nine months had elapsed without another break, I boasted to my friend Koziol: "I'm on my way to heaven."

But it was not meant to be.

CHAPTER EIGHT

• • • • • • • • • • • • • • • • • •

Ghosts

Once more our Lord was asleep on the boat.
—St. Teresa of the Child of Jesus

The morning of August 1, 1944, started in the usual, monotonous school-vacation fashion: Wait for your turn at the toilet, scrub hands and face with gritty laundry soap, remember the ears, brush teeth with index finger and the same foul-tasting soap, slip on the threadbare gray dress with the frayed white collar that we all wear every day, line up, march to prayers.

Chores: On this day, mine was sweeping the dormitory. An older girl supervised, rapping us with a ruler if we forgot to sprinkle the floor with water to keep the dust down or to reach far enough under each bed.

Breakfast: A slice of black bread with oily tasting margarine. Tea with a drop of milk.

Potato peeling: Eight of us at a time, seated around a bulging burlap sack and speckled enamel tub. Dull, stubby knives scraping against callused fingers. Check each potato for remaining eyes. Plop, plop as potatoes hit the water, like the patter of rain.

It was, in fact, raining—a drizzly rain, more like a mist, and when Marysia appeared for an unexpected visit, her old black coat smelled of damp wool. During the school year, she came only on Sundays, after church, but in the summer she might show up anytime, as she did today, rescuing me from a mountain of potatoes.

"It's raining," said Sister Magdalena, who signed people out for visits. She was a pleasant, smiling nun who took a personal interest in her charges. "You usually go to the park. What will you do on this rainy day?"

"My cousin in the Old Town invited us to her name-day party," Marysia lied, which told me this would be one of those special occasions when I would be visiting my parents.

"Well, take your overcoat or you'll get soaked," Sister Magdalena advised.

I owned one coat. My parents had acquired it last autumn from a friend whose daughter had died of diphtheria. It was too large, and Marysia had filled it with goose down for the winter. Not very comfortable on a stifling August day, but one did not argue with a nun. I went to the well-swept dorm and pulled the coat out of the crate under my bed. In a farewell gesture, Marysia and I kissed the sister's hand, right on the wedding ring that signifies her betrothal to Christ.

"Be back before dark." Sister Magdalena waved as we left the convent.

● ● ● ● ●

Visits to my parents were rare, no more than once a month, and never disclosed to me in advance. As with all other information, the less I knew, the less I could inadvertently spill. Why this particular day was chosen I did not know. I didn't even think to ask. Perhaps nobody knew. There are things not given to us to know.

My mother was expecting us and left the door to the apartment slightly ajar—if we didn't have to waste time ringing doorbells, we would be less likely to run into snooping neighbors. We tiptoed upstairs. My mother laughed at me in the winter coat and hung it in the closet. The apartment sizzled in the heat. My mother's face and neck glistened with sweat. The Countess refused to open windows; she caught colds easily, she claimed, and feared for her weak heart.

Now, as usual, she lay in bed, tucked under several covers. Despite her fragile health, Lady Vala cut an imposing figure. Years later, when I first saw Katharine Hepburn, I was reminded of the Countess's long neck and upright, regal bearing. She stemmed from nobility and carried this heritage with pride. Her pale face with its sculpted features set off the sparkling sapphire of her eyes. Wavy white hair rippled down to her waist. She loved to have my parents, especially my father, comb it with her fine-toothed ivory comb. He had a magic touch that never failed to comfort her.

I greeted the Countess, shaking a clammy hand and kissing her rubbery cheek. Then, while Marysia busied herself with mending, I hugged my mother and, in response to her questions, babbled on about convent life.

"What did you have for breakfast?" my mother asked.

"Yucky bread. But do you want to see how I can make it taste better?" I demonstrated squeezing and rolling a chunk of bread between my fingers. "It clumps into a hard, chewy ball."

"You shouldn't play with your food," my mother chided. "Did you finish it all?"

She, like the nuns, worried about my poor appetite.

"Oh, yes!" A lie to bring to confession.

"Well, I have something for lunch today that you'll love."

"What?"

"You'll see. First tell me what's new at the convent."

"Nothing."

I wanted so much to tell her how close I was getting to reaching salvation, but the subject of my Catholicism was best left alone. Any enthusiasm I showed about religious life evoked a faraway gaze that made me feel as if Mama had disappeared. And so, with my mother, I kept quiet about being a Catholic, just as in other situations I kept quiet about being a Jew.

"Did you make any new friends?" Mama asked, offering a new topic.

"No," I said. "I still mostly play with Koziol. But she was

horrible today. She sat next to me in potato-peeling, and every time Sister looked away, she tossed her potato into the water so hard, it would splash me all over." I could hear my voice getting whiny. "She did it on purpose, just to be mean!"

It felt good to complain to my mother. I thought of another subject.

"And I hardly slept at all last night."

"Why? There wasn't any air raid."

"A ghost," I said.

"Oh?"

"It was just after lights out. Zosia felt a ghost under her bed and so she jumped out and then Koziol jumped out of bed and she sleeps right next to me, so then the ghost got under my bed. I was so scared, I never . . ."

"What made you think it was . . ."

"A ghost? Don't you know how you can tell? Well, the way you know is your mattress starts lifting up and down like there was somebody wiggling around under it."

"I see," my mother said. "Did you jump out of bed, too?"

"Sure! And then the ghost started moving around under everybody's beds and we were all screaming and running out in the hall. And then Sister Clementine came with a flashlight and looked under all the beds and the ghost was gone."

"Do you really think . . ."

"So then Sister made us all kneel down and pray and then we went to bed again. But I just slept with my eyes open all night, I was so scared the ghost would come back."

"Is it possible you just imagined . . . ."

I could tell she didn't believe me. My father would believe

me, I thought. But where was he? Basking in the warmth of Mama's undivided attention, I realized only now that I had not seen him yet.

"Where is Tatus?" Ever since the Gestapo caught my mother, I worried when either of them was absent.

"He went to meet someone," my mother answered. "He'll be back soon and said we could start eating without him."

All right, I thought. I'll have Mama and Marysia to myself a little longer. My father had a way of filling whatever space he occupied. We settled down to lunch, while the Countess dropped off to sleep in her bedroom.

My mother opened the icebox and pulled out the surprise. In my honor she had obtained two slices of ham—another food gift from the German officer next door. I had not acquired my Babcia's distaste for pork; ham was my very favorite food. Mama arranged the two slices on a platter, as if there were enough to fill it. We all laughed. Marysia fried some mashed-potato pancakes and poured me a glass of buttermilk. The pancakes were for all of us, but the ham and milk were just for me. I felt very important. It was a feast, and as I relaxed into it I could feel my sluggish appetite perk up.

Two gunshots interrupted the party. They rang out right under our windows. The crystal chandeliers trembled and tinkled. Shouts reached us from the street. The terror that always struck me during air raids gripped me now. I almost choked on the ham still in my mouth. Marysia and I both jumped and started for the window, but my mother said no, the panes can splinter. I looked to her to do something, but for a frightening moment she just sat there, paralyzed.

"Tatus," she said in a barely audible voice. "He is still gone."

Usually she counted on my father to make critical decisions. And he had not yet returned. Seconds later, a whole volley of shots pierced the air. Glass shattered somewhere nearby. A faint smell of smoke filtered in despite the closed windows. Finally my mother sprang into action. She looked out a window, crouching under it to avoid broken glass.

"There's a fire. We have to get out."

Marysia ran to wake Lady Vala. My mother grabbed a scarf, her cigarette case, my coat. Grasping my arm, she dashed for the front door. Marysia pulled along the groggy Countess.

"No, no," the Countess protested. "You go. Leave me here. I don't have the strength."

"You do, you do," Marysia coaxed. "God will help you."

"But where is the Doctor?" the Countess whimpered. My father's absence hung over all of us like a shadow.

My mother tore open the door to the outside hallway. A thick, acrid cloud assaulted us, stinging our throats, scratching our eyes. Coughing and crying, I could see the stairwell belch black smoke, laced with flames licking up from below.

"Oh sweet Jesus!" Marysia exclaimed. "There's no way we can make it down the stairs."

My mother, fortunately, proved equal to the crisis.

"Check the back exit," she yelled, and slammed the front door shut.

We raced to the kitchen, from which a rarely used staircase led down to the backyard. The smoke on this stairwell was still translucent. We piled down the stairs. My mother, clutching my hand, was in the lead. When I started to choke, she tossed me her scarf to cover my face. Marysia followed behind, urging on the Countess, whose coughing was punctuated by explosions from the street.

In the backyard, next to the trash barrels, the janitor lay in a pool of blood. I had noticed this man on previous visits, sweeping the hall, polishing the mahogany banisters. He had smiled at me going up the stairs with Marysia and asked no questions. Once Lady Vala called him to fix a broken hinge, and I heard his deep voice from behind the closed door of the room where we stayed when outsiders came.

The janitor was dead. I could tell by the way his body was sprawled out like a rag. I had never seen a dead person before. A queasy, nauseous feeling stirred in my stomach, but there was no time to react further. My mother was leading us out of the backyard and into the street.

We stopped momentarily to look around. Neighbors were pouring out of their buildings. Flames were leaping from one dwelling to the next. But across the street, there was no fire. Mama, squeezing my wrist until it hurt, joined the throngs rushing to the other side. Behind us, Marysia dragged the reluctant Countess, whose rasping breath reassured me that Marysia was close by.

We stepped over bodies littering the street. They already emanated a sickly sweet smell that was to infect the air for months. Bullets whistled over our heads. German tanks were rolling in, and small boys were pelting them with bottles of gasoline.

We reached an air-raid shelter just before a bomb hit and demolished several buildings on the side of the street we had just left. In the crowded basement, we heard planes roaring overhead, releasing several bombs at a time.

"It's the Uprising," the huddled refugees whispered.

• • • • •

The Warsaw Uprising* had begun. Sixty-three days later, the capital of Poland would lay in ruins, with no one but ghosts left to stumble over the rubble.

---

* The Warsaw Uprising, starting August 1, 1944, should be distinguished from the earlier Warsaw Ghetto Uprising, which occurred in the spring of 1943. The Warsaw Uprising pitted Polish insurgents against the Germans, while the Warsaw Ghetto Uprising was an attempt of the Jews to break out of the ghetto.

Chapter 8

CHAPTER NINE

. . . .

The Warsaw Uprising

in the fire-depths
saw the way
a peony crumbles
—Kato Shuson

The web of basements across the street sheltered us for three days. Mostly what I remember is running, from one basement to another, to a third, back to the first, and around again. Each in turn would burst into flames.

There was almost no food. A neighbor shared her only loaf of bread. I wasn't hungry; fear filled my belly. I looked to my mother for comfort, but she hardly saw me. She focused only on the hope that my father was still alive.

News from the outside filtered in with the continuing stream of refugees from surrounding buildings. Some had access to radios and "underground" news broadcasts.

"The minute the Uprising started," one of them said, "the Germans swept all pedestrians off the streets."

"What happened to them?"

"Shot."

In the dark basement, it is always night.

"Go to sleep," Mama says.

I roll up into a ball inside the circle of her arms. My body shakes with her sobs, and my face stings with her tears. In the dim light of a kerosene lantern, her swollen eyelids bulge over eyes that stare absently into the dark.

"If only he hadn't gone out," she moans. "I shouldn't have let him. We all knew the Uprising was brewing."

Marysia and the Countess fade into the background. I lock entirely into my mother. And she is dwindling away from me.

"If he is dead," she says, "I want to die, too."

⬤ ⬤ ⬤ ⬤ ⬤

In the shelter, spirits lifted with the rumor that the Russians would soon arrive. The Polish insurgents had dared to challenge the Germans on the strength of the Soviet Union's promise to help. Russian troops had already broken through to Praga, a city on the outskirts of Warsaw. In another day or two, we thought, the Uprising would be over.

As each new arrival tumbled into the shelter with a pale, frightened face, the group would pounce with questions:

"The Russians?"

"Not yet."

By the fourth day, the fire had spread uncontrollably throughout the maze of interconnected basements. We had to vacate the shelter. As we climbed out, the sunlight blinded me. I followed the grownups to the second story of a partially bombed-out building next door. It felt good to breathe fresh air.

Squinting in the sunlight, we stared at the flames leaping from broken windows all around us. We scanned the rubble for a sign of Russian tanks. No Russians. Instead, the next day, our second-story hideout was discovered by the Germans. Their heavy boots kicked in the door.

"All men out!" they shouted, prodding the ten or so men with the butts of their rifles. One man fell down and I heard the crack of a rifle on his skull. The women and children remained behind. There was no screaming. Just silence as the women watched their men get loaded onto a truck. For the first time in almost a week, Mama was almost smiling.

"If he had stayed with us," she said, "they would have taken him now. Maybe God meant to save him. At least there is a chance."

Two days later, the Russians still lingered on the outskirts of Warsaw. The Germans returned to our "hideout." I looked at my mother's face; it was drawn tight. I grasped Marysia's hand, and she pulled me close. I felt her tremble. Terror boiled in my belly. Were we going to die?

But God was good.

"You women and children will go to the Polish sector,"

one of the Nazis barked. He stomped on the floor. Schnell, schnell. "Hurry, hurry." We grabbed our few possessions and poured down the stairs.

The Polish sector was a detroyed part of Warsaw that the Polish insurgents had managed to hold. We never did understand why the Germans chose to let us go, rather than kill us. They did kill all of the men.

•　•　•　•　•

And so again we run, the women and children, my mother squeezing my wrist, dragging me, Marysia dragging the Countess. We trip over ruins and detour around barricades constructed from the debris of bombed-out houses. Shots erupt all around us. The street is strewn with corpses. If you hold your breath, you can get by the stink of rotting flesh.

I've never run so fast. The summer heat burns in my chest. My mouth feels parched, my legs wobbly, but I keep up with my mother's frantic strides. We reach some sort of boundary. Polish insurgents let us through their barricades.

•　•　•　•　•

The next fifty-eight days form a choppy patchwork of isolated memories:

Twelve people in a small room. We are living with a friend of a friend—something like that. By the light of a single bare bulb, the women are examining their underwear. Bras, girdles, panties, and slips come under scrutiny. Marysia helps me with mine. My mother sits back watching.

"How about you?" One of the women challenges her.

Polish rebels building barricades during the Warsaw Uprising, August 1944.

"Aren't you joining us?"

"I don't have fleas," Mama responds, pulling herself up straight.

"Of course not," the woman says, to a chorus of laughter. "No flea would dare settle on your aristocratic body!"

My mother bows to the pressure. She removes her underclothes.

"I have fleas," she admits. More laughter accompanies the snap of fleas being squashed between twelve sets of thumbnails.

"The Russians are sitting on our doorstep but still haven't come to help us," one of the women says, when the laughter dies down. "What's holding them up?"

Nobody knows.

● ● ● ● ●

Bombs fall on the Polish-held sector, too, and city services have been disrupted. We need water, and nearby is a functioning well. My mother hands me a small pail and takes a big one for herself. She grasps my free hand as we scurry the half-mile to the well. Explosions and the ever-present stench of death accompany us. Despite the fear that has by now settled deep within me, I enjoy this excursion. I pretend that I am the Swiss girl Heidi fetching water for her goats. We reach the well. Mama pumps the long handle, and clear water squirts into her pail.

I am fascinated. I have never seen a well before.

"Can I pump my own?" I beg. "Please?"

She lets me, despite the danger. We are sharing a moment of fun. With full pails, we start back, unable to run now. The water sloshes around, and some spills on my shoes. My mother gives me a disapproving look, but she does not scold.

"It's OK," she says. "Just do the best you can."

The pail is heavy, its handle cutting into my palm. I see my mother struggling with hers as well; this gives me courage to plod on. We shift sides along the way. Somehow we make it back.

Marysia rushes out to relieve me of my burden.

"What a trouper you are!" she beams at me. My chest swells with pride.

That evening the whole lot of us takes sponge baths in a big tin tub. I go last, after all the adults have had a turn. By this time, the harsh brown laundry soap has turned the bath a muddy mustard. Still, the bath feels like pure luxury.

* * * * *

The Russians continued to tarry on the outskirts of Warsaw. It seemed that they could have easily marched in to help the Polish insurgents to defeat the Germans, as had been promised by Stalin. But they did not do so.

Poland, the adults complained bitterly, has been betrayed. My mother's face flushed with anger as she spat out the name Stalin. Her anger soothed me. I preferred it to the tears that she still shed for my father every night. The prospect of his having survived dimmed with each report of German atrocities against the population.

The German bombers emitted an ear-piercing wail a minute or two before the bombs fell. Seven bombs were dropped simultaneously. The bombs followed the wail with the same inevitability that thunder follows lightning. In the moments between the signal and the strike, we always dashed down to the basement. The Countess, daily more frail and frozen with fear, generally staggered down at the end of the line.

* * * * *

The Countess is lying in bed. The bomber whine starts. We all take off for the basement, but she refuses to budge.

"Come on," my mother yells. Marysia tries to pull off her covers.

"No!" The Countess is adamant. "I'm not going. I can't."

Only seconds remain before the bombs will fall. There is no choice. We have to leave her. She remains upstairs, alone. From the basement we hear seven explosions. The walls shake, but the building is not hit.

When we return to the apartment, Countess Valentina Mlodecka is absolutely still. She has died of fright.

I liked the word "Allies." It sounded comforting, like "ice cream." "British" and "American": pleasant words, too. The Russians were not helping us, my mother said, but the Allies would. The Allies, according to radio news reports, possibly from BBC or Voice of America, were air-dropping supplies to the Polish insurgents. With this help, we felt sure, victory was only days away.

But the Allied supplies fell mostly into German hands. The Russians refused to let Allied planes land in their airfields. The Allies gave up the rescue mission. And again the Poles were on their own.

•　•　•　•　•

My mother, Marysia, and I are on the run again. From bombs? From Germans? I don't remember.

Mama pounds on the door of an acquaintance. A woman, Mrs. Kogut (which means "rooster"), peeks through

Civilians herded to labor camps after the Warsaw Uprising, October 1944.

a keyhole. She lets us in and bolts the door. Mrs. Kogut, a Christian, knows that we are Jews. Her husband is tossing around on a cot by the window. He is drunk. Mrs. Kogut pulls down the shades. Mr. Kogut is yelling, "Plaster, plaster, I need plaster!" He scratches at the wall and licks the plaster caught under his fingernails.

"He always wants plaster when he drinks," Mrs. Kogut whispers in explanation. "His body craves it."

She motions us to a couch and warns us to be quiet. We must not attract her husband's attention. Mrs. Kogut says that we can stay only until nightfall—we must leave before her husband wakes up. He hates Jews and would call the police. I'm squeezed in on the couch between my mother and Marysia. Mama's body is tight. Marysia is fingering her rosaries. I know that the drunken man's screams can alert the police. We sit like statues while Mr. Kogut, the "rooster," crows for plaster.

•　•　•　•　•

August 1944 turns into September, September into October. On the first morning of October, I wake to a rush of excitement.

"The Polish insurgents have capitulated," my mother hastily explains. "Warsaw is back in German hands."

She hurries me out of bed. The Germans have ordered the Poles to come out immediately into the street. We must carry white cloths to show that we are surrendering. Mama hands me my coat and a white pillowcase to wave over my head. She and Marysia grab sheets. In the street, people are pouring out of every building, all carrying their white symbols of defeat. German soldiers are directing everyone to a central location.

Like a macabre procession of ghosts, the white-shrouded crowd stumbles over the debris. My mother holds my hand. We walk for what seems like forever. Finally we arrive at a large market square. Here we are told to wait. We stand, and wait. And wait. Frost is already forming on the rubble around us. Women still wearing summer dresses are shivering. I am grateful for my heavy coat. My feet hurt.

Chapter 9

Whispers bounce between the members of the group.

"What will they do to us now?"

My feet hurt so much that I welcome the sight of the SS man charged with our fate. He begins a "selection"—for what, we do not know.

"All men on this side!"

The men shuffle over to the right side of the square. The SS guard scans the remaining people.

"If you are a woman with a child, stand here!"

He watches carefully to make sure that only women with children move to the left. My mother and I join a small group, perhaps thirty in all. Marysia still stands in the center of the square. I am ready to scream. I won't go without her. The scream tears soundlessly at my throat.

"Sick women, very sick women," the SS guard barks. "Are there any sick women here?"

Marysia timorously raises her arm.

"I have a heart condition," she says, which is true. She pulls out some sort of medical card.

"Over there!" the guard points to our group. Marysia and three or four other women join us. I can hardly contain my joy. I don't know what will happen to us. But at least we're together. And the Warsaw Uprising is over.

CHAPTER 10

. . . .

A Moment of Childhood

One joy scatters a hundred griefs.
—Chinese proverb

A convoy of open trucks swallowed up the men and the healthy women without children. The trucks roared off—to labor or concentration camps, we were to learn—while our small huddle watched and waited, the white sheets and scraps of fabric wrapped around us. I imagine that husbands were ripped away from their wives, fathers from their children. I imagine tears and shouts and pleas, although I don't remember them. My father, of course, was not there.

After the convoy departed, three more empty trucks pulled up. They were there for the rest of us. The Germans growled orders, counting off: *Eins, zwei, drei . . . .*

Fifteen or so people piled into the first truck. They peered behind them, watching the next batch, including Marysia, my mother, and me, climb into the middle truck. Marysia got in first, and Mama hoisted me up into Marysia's outstretched arms. Then my mother herself scaled the slippery side of the tall vehicle, grasping the muddy tire to pull herself up. The women squeezed closer together, jostled one another, to make room for us. We settled into a rear corner and watched the rest of the group fill the last truck behind us.

Despite the grim silence of the passengers, broken only by occasional guttural German from the guards, I felt in a holiday mood. Having lived in cities all my life, I had never ridden in an open truck before. This was going to be fun!

A Nazi soldier jumped aboard. In broken Polish, he told us that we were going to a place called Mstow. We shouldn't worry, he said; we would be safe there. I looked at my mother to see if this was good or bad news. She gave me a cautious smile and hugged me. Her body felt more relaxed than usual, so I breathed more easily. Having given his brief bulletin, the German started marching around the crowded truckbed, stumbling over people, unceremoniously kicking anyone in his path. He asked our names and wrote them down on a pad, using a new sheet of paper for each person.

He stopped in front of my mother.

"Pola Kaliszewska," she said, giving her assumed name. She pulled out her identification papers, but the German waved them away. He seemed to be in a rush. Obviously he did not suspect us of being Jewish. He pointed at me.

"Teresa Chrystyna Kaliszewska," my mother said. I

glanced at her with a start. Wasn't I Teresa Chrystyna Urban anymore? My mother looked away from me, which I gathered meant to ask no questions. I tried to figure it out. I guessed we had entered a new phase. My mother was now officially my mother, and I, as her daughter, would clearly bear her name. Why could I now be her daughter? I whispered the new name under my breath. It sounded strange and not like me at all. I had gotten used to Teresa Chrystyna Urban.

The German jumped off the truck and slipped into the front seat of the cab, beside the driver. Horns sounded, and the three trucks lurched forward. The October wind blew hard, and the women scooted down low and held onto their scarves. I snuggled tight between Mama and Marysia, who tucked me under the winter coat from the convent. I loved the feel of the wind sweeping my cheeks, slapping my braids against my neck. Less adventurous passengers made windshields out of their white linens.

We wound through the devastated streets of Warsaw, frequently detouring around mountains of rubble. Over the side of the truck, I stared into the gaping mouths of gutted buildings. Charred wall fragments. Crumbling staircases. Caved-in roofs. Most structures were leveled to the ground.

Finally we reached the outskirts of the city, entering a rural, pastoral terrain. Bony cows were grazing in the fields, and haystacks dotted the dry grass. An occasional farmer clattered by in his horse-and-buggy. A couple of little boys in the truck behind us peeped out over the sides and started waving to us. I joined in the game.

A sudden commotion in our vehicle—whispers, women stretching their necks to look—alerted me that something was happening: The lead truck had turned off in a different direction. We lost sight of it. Absorbed in my game, I continued to wave to the children behind us, but suddenly their vehicle, too, veered off. Its sharp turn toppled the little boys. They disappeared from view. Seconds later, so did their truck.

Fear now spread through our group. It was as if everyone had taken a deep sigh and now couldn't let out their breath. I felt my mother tremble, and Marysia pulled out her rosaries. Why were we separated from the other two trucks? we all were wondering. Who was going where? I lost interest in the scenery and crumpled into a ball, hugging my knees. A silence settled on the group as no answers came forth.

The hushed atmosphere relaxed a bit when a passenger spotted a giant stork's nest perched atop a farmhouse. She announced her discovery and I popped up to look. The stork's nest gave birth to jokes I didn't understand, but I laughed because the others were laughing.

The ride through the countryside was fairly smooth, as the area had not been bombed. Little chapels, featuring statues of the Holy Mother, bordered the road. Marysia crossed herself and said a prayer as we passed each one. I followed suit. If my mother noticed, she did not object.

Some road signs were still standing. Marysia, who could not read, asked me what they said. With my second-grade education, I could decipher most of the signs, but one long word had me stumped.

"What does that say?" I asked Mama, who was now gazing listlessly at the horizon.

I had to ask twice, but finally she replied, "Czestochowa."

Marysia was thrilled.

"Czestochowa!" she exclaimed. She had always wanted to make a pilgrimage to the famous shrine towering on a hill in this city. Jasna Gora, the shrine was called: "Mountain of Light."

"Thousands of pilgrims travel there each day to ask help of the Black Madonna," Marysia said.

"Black Madonna?"

"Yes. In the holiest part of the shrine hangs the beautiful painting of the Madonna holding Baby Jesus. Their faces are black. The Black Madonna saved Poland from invaders long ago. And she answers the prayers of all the pilgrims who climb the mountain to see her." Many people have been known to throw away their crutches on the strenuous trek up to the shrine, Marysia explained. "Oh, I hope we will go and pray for the safety of our loved ones."

A woman sitting close to us joined the conversation.

"My husband and I got married at the shrine," she said. "So many couples, all in white, all kneeling before the Holy Mother." She fell silent. Her husband was one of the men just taken away by the Germans. "We had a good marriage," she said.

Another woman told of a friend who left her crutches by the altar. And still another explained that the blessed painting was executed on a wooden board taken from the home of Jesus in Nazareth.

I had never seen Marysia cry, but now tears filled her eyes. I thought about her family, and I thought about my father. I too wanted to kneel at the shrine of the Madonna who cured the lame and who once saved all of Poland.

The truck, however, swerved off the main road and bounced along on a muddy country lane.

"Is this Jasna Gora?" I asked, excited by the sight of a big church on a hill.

"No," Marysia replied and her eyes were sad. "*Jasna Gora* is much, much bigger than that."

Moments later we crossed a rickety, narrow bridge. A small sign on the other side of it proclaimed "Mstow" (pronounced Mstoov).

We pulled into a little village square. To me, having always been in cities, everything seemed in miniature, like a town for dolls. Small houses with thatched roofs. Tiny stores: a bakery, a dentist's office, a tobacco and candy shop, a shoemaker. A few old men relaxed on benches in a small park, feeding birds.

As our truck roared into this sleepy town, the residents began to stream out of every corner. A band of children, unafraid, ran to cluster around us. The German guard motioned us off the truck. We hopped off, wobbly and dazed. The children surrounded us with squeals of laughter. Several had brought gifts. A little girl, about my size, handed me a teddy bear no bigger than my thumb. Another shyly offered three embroidered flowers. Others gave me colorful paper stickers of angels and a dainty soft handkerchief. What a wonderful welcome!

The adults of the village, more cautious than their offspring, huddled together some distance from the truck. They looked at us with curiosity and, probably, suspicion. Strangers rarely disturbed the routine of life in this sleepy place. Apart from a stray visitor, perhaps a pilgrim lost on the way to Jasna Gora, outsiders would have little cause to stop in Mstow. Nothing new had happened here in years. Even the war seemed far away—having no military value, Mstow had not been bombed. But the war barged into town now, in the form of a truckful of Warsaw refugees.

Poor, uneducated, and fearful of strangers, the villagers had been ordered to absorb this remnant of the Warsaw population. The other two truckloads that had started out with us had been routed to two similar farm villages elsewhere. But we did not know this at the time.

Why did the Germans choose to offer us a safe haven? Perhaps releasing people who most likely could not work hard in a labor camp provided the Nazis with a cover of "humanitarianism." But really nobody knew. The Germans who had murdered the vast majority of Warsaw citizens, Jews and Christians alike, the Germans who deported to camps most of the few survivors of the Uprising—these Germans had chosen to offer shelter to approximately fifty women and children. And Marysia, my mother, and I were among them.

Commotion ensued as the guard assigned members of our group to different citizens of Mstow. The residents of the village, many illiterate, were milling around, peering at the papers given them by the Germans. Some approached the

Warsaw women, asking them to decipher the names. The Warsaw group looked around in confusion, not really understanding what was supposed to happen. Meanwhile, the guard returned to the truck, which took off, leaving us and the townspeople standing in the middle of the square.

I hardly noticed what the adults were doing, since the children, still fascinated with the new arrivals, took turns holding my hand, leading me around the square, inviting me to a game of hopscotch. One girl wanted to play catch, but when she threw the ball, I dropped it. I had never learned to play ball.

Slowly the adults began to sort it all out. An elderly woman in a flowered housedress and black shawl introduced herself to Mama and Marysia. She was holding the three papers on which our names were written. I reluctantly parted with my new friends to shake the woman's hand, and the three of us followed her to a small shack around the corner from the square. It had a thatched roof and a gate that opened into a backyard, where a few chickens scampered away when they saw us. Inside, the home boasted a kitchen and an all-purpose living room/bedroom. A sort of foyer abutted this room.

"You will sleep here," the woman, Magda, pointed to a pile of straw in the foyer. A thick goosedown throw lay at the foot of this makeshift bed. "It's not much," she apologized, "but it's warm and . . . ."

"Oh, please," my mother interrupted. "We are very grateful to you."

"God bless you," Marysia added.

"I live here alone," the woman said. "My husband passed away not even a year ago. The house feels so empty. I will be happy for your company."

Our hostess flipped through the papers handed her by the German guard. She pored over them, squinting to make out the words.

"I see that you will be taking your meals with other families. I'm sorry, but I . . . I am a poor widow," she started to apologize again, as if we were the ones doing her a favor.

Marysia, Magda explained, would be having meals with another widow, Mrs. Golub. My mother and I would be eating with the Kamienickis. They had children for me to play with, she told us. Magda offered to show us the way to these two homes.

We dropped Marysia off first and then walked back to the village square. Facing the square stood a whitewashed house, somewhat bigger than most. Inside, Mr. and Mrs. Kamienicki greeted us, literally with open arms. They were a warm, cheerful couple—he with a thin face, a wispy blonde mustache, a couple of missing teeth; she plump and dimpled, with pink cheeks and a round, smiling face. An older man, hunchbacked, observed us from a distance.

"Children," Mrs. Kamienicki called after the introductions. "Our guests are here."

Three girls materialized, one bigger and two smaller than myself. They hung back shyly, hiding and giggling behind their mother.

"Dora, Ania, and Basia," Mrs. Kamienicki introduced them, starting with the biggest. She pulled them out from behind her back. "Come on, you know how to behave," she scolded, and the girls, politely though with downcast eyes, shook hands with my mother. Dora took off, but the younger two stayed, looking me over.

"Want to play cards?" the middle one offered, but now it was my turn to be shy. I shook my head.

"We are pleased that you will be taking meals with us," Mrs. Kamienicki said. "I hope you will like my cooking."

My mother started to thank her, but she cut her off with a laugh. "You can see I enjoy my cooking," Mrs. Kamienicki kidded, patting her substantial belly.

"I hope I can repay your kindness," my mother said. "What can I do to help?"

Again Mrs. Kamienicki laughed.

"You look like a fine city lady, "she said, taking my mother's soft hands into her callused ones. "You are not used to chopping wood and hauling water like we farmers are."

"I guess not," my mother admitted. "But I would like to do something."

"Can you knit?" Mr. Kamienicki, who had stood by quietly, suddenly asked with a burst of laughter.

"Yes, of course," my mother said, though I had never seen her do it.

"Then maybe you can knit a sweater for my father."

The old man in the corner chuckled. "Who can knit for a hunchback?" he grumbled.

"I can," my mother said. And the very next day she bought several skeins of dark green wool.

* * * * *

Seven months elapsed between our arrival in Mstow and the end of the war. That winter, in February 1945, I turned nine. Protected by its backwardness and insignificance, the village continued its normal routines. Thus I received the gift of carefree childhood, a reprieve. While the Nazis systematically wiped out whatever was still standing in Warsaw and tortured, starved, shot, gassed, and burned Jews in ever more staggering numbers, I played tag, hopscotch, roll-the-hoop, hide and seek. Mostly I played with Ania and Basia. Sometimes Dora joined, but usually she chose to declare her superiority. She called me a big baby and more than once reduced me to tears. She had no patience to teach me games. I complained to my mother, who said that Dora was jealous to have another girl in the house.

At school, equipped with my convent education, I outshone my peers in the third grade. With admiration, they asked me to help them figure their sums on small black chalkboards.

On Sundays, Marysia, my mother, and I joined our neighbors in church. I took communion but no longer counted the number needed for salvation. Salvation doesn't come until death, and thoughts of death took a back seat in the peaceful farm life around me. From various neighbors, I learned about nature. I learned to place glasses of milk, still warm from the cow, on the windowsill and watch how the cream rose to the top. The rest of the milk would harden into a smooth, yogurt-like gel, a delicious brew called sour milk. I learned to skim the cream and churn it into butter in a big wooden tub. A newborn goat somehow appeared at Magda's door, and she let me feed it with a baby bottle.

Mstow—a village.

Despite the cold, snowy winter, life seemed to bloom all around me, so that even death itself lost its terrors. One time, while running through the square, my friends and I were startled by a sight in the shoemaker's window. A corpse, all decked out in black suit and black shoes, lay stretched out on a table in the window, as if he were a dummy modeling the shoes. None of us knew him, although one girl thought he was the shoemaker's uncle. We huddled together and whispered and giggled, but the nervousness passed and none of us was afraid.

I was free of fear in those months, perhaps for the very first time. Bombs never crashed here. Air-raid sirens rarely blared. I heard no marital arguments. And no one suspected us of being Jews—if we looked different from the local people, so did the rest of the big-city folk who had descended on the village from Warsaw.

I soon got accustomed to my latest name: Kaliszewska was not so bad, I thought. It was actually nice having the same name as my mother. Urban was not my real name, anyway.

And what was my real name? Hopping on a haywagon with my school friend, Renia, I really didn't care. What mattered was the tumbling and laughing and covering each other with hay, while Renia's toothless grandpa delivered shining silver canisters of fresh milk to his customers around town.

Among the smells of farm life I remember straw the best—the straw mattress on which we slept. The straw crackled under my knees as I knelt to say my evening prayers. Then I would scoot under the covers, and later on I would breathe in the sweet smell of the straw mingled with the warm, sweaty scents of Mama and Marysia, each lying on either side of me. I was safe and warm tucked in between them, my two mothers.

They were with me during the day, too. Marysia sewed dresses for me, since we had brought almost nothing from Warsaw. I had left what little I had in the convent. I remember a summery, short-sleeved dress in gray and white checks, with puffed sleeves and a scalloped Peter Pan collar. And a beautiful sailor dress with a large hem that my mother would let out for several years to come. Just like in Przemysl, I watched Marysia's fingers fly over the cloth and her foot press the pedal as I listened to the soft purr of Magda's dilapidated Singer sewing machine. I would read to Marysia, stories of Polish heroes in thin booklets that we could borrow from school. The booklets were tattered from years of use, and there were maybe four or five copies for a class of thirty. Marysia loved to listen, sometimes even as she sewed. It was only many years later that I found out how my father, as a child, had read to Marysia's mother, Kasia. And Marysia taught me a little about sewing, so that I could thread the needle and the bobbin, and stitch together straight sides.

I did my homework with Mama. She gave French lessons to a couple of teenage girls in Mstow and I would sit in. She assigned a hundred vocabulary words per week to her pupils, and I worked harder under her tutelage than at school. She also taught me how to knit. With scraps of wool from the green sweater that she was making for old Mr. Kamienicki, I fashioned one for my new little teddy bear. And we played cards, too. She taught me krapet, the double-solitaire game she used to play with my father. I was getting accustomed to her presence now; after so many years of being apart, I treasured every minute of our time together.

The only cloud on the sunny horizon during this time was my mother's grief. She still cried at night, though less often each month; in the morning I would taste salty streaks when I kissed her cheeks. I wondered why she missed my father so much, and what I could do to make up for him. I tried to be as undemanding as possible, not even to ask for kisses unless she offered them. I straightened up our room, picking up stray stalks of straw and stuffing them back in the mattress. I offered to play krapet every day, even though I usually lost. I tried to get perfect grades in school and to memorize the hundred French vocabulary words more quickly than the other pupils.

To be truthful, I was jealous of the place my father occupied in my mother's heart. For me, after the years of separation, he had become a vague shadow. And I could not forget the arguments between them—nor the panicked way he had greeted me when I arrived in Warsaw. One day, as I snuggled in my mother's lap like a much younger child, I realized with a pang of guilt that I was glad to have her all to myself.

And then one day, in April 1945, the war was over. Perhaps the Black Madonna had saved Poland again, I thought. Several camouflaged trucks roared into town, and a small contingent of Russian soldiers spilled out. They wore bedraggled khaki uniforms with little caps like upside-down paper boats. Their boots were worn and muddy, nothing like the fearsome German boots, which were always polished to a shine. Rifles were slung over their shoulders. The soldiers scattered over the streets, milling around the village, while all of us ran out to welcome them. There was laughing and shouting and weeping at the sight of the liberators for whom we had been waiting for so long. Women threw their arms around these very young, tired soldiers, men kissed them on both cheeks, and children hopped and danced.

My mother, with me in tow, approached a soldier standing by himself, a bored expression on his face. She enthusiastically pumped his hand.

"How wonderful to see you!" she exclaimed. He barely nodded in response.

Just then several German planes streaked across the sky, and we heard explosions. The retreating Germans were dumping their deadly cargoes of bombs even as they fled. The streets emptied, everyone running for cover. My mother pulled me into the church. Through the open door we saw the soldier still rooted to the spot where we had left him. The planes passed, and we ventured back out.

"Why didn't you go inside?" Mama asked the soldier, pointing to the church in case he didn't understand her Polish. "You could have gotten killed out here."

"I'm not afraid to die," he said in Russian.

The two languages are similar, and I understood. I looked at him in surprise. His face was blank. It made me sad. My mother seemed sad, too, and angry.

"That's how the Soviet Army trains its men," she said to me gruffly on the way home. "Not to care if they live or die."

I wondered why this soldier, a total stranger, had upset her so. Later that evening she asked, "Do you remember your Uncle Artur? He was just about that soldier's age when we saw him last."

I remembered a handsome, playful young man who would burst into song: "I invited my honey to meet me at nine . . ."

"You know," my mother continued, without waiting for

an answer. "I was hoping that perhaps he escaped to Russia. And maybe joined the Russian Army. There was something about that soldier . . . for a minute I thought . . ."

"When will we see Uncle Artur?" I asked. Mama sighed deeply.

"I don't know, darling. Now that the war is over, I hope he will return. He and your Tatus. Let's pray that they are both alive."

She drew me to her and we sat quietly. Perhaps she was praying. But in her silence I heard words she wouldn't utter. Words that meant that her brother, who cared so much about life, would never come back. Neither he nor my father.

But God was listening—at least with one ear.

●　●　●　●　●

We were still in Mstow a month or so after the war had ended. Despite the departure of the Nazis, Mama and I continued to live under our assumed names and to hide the fact that we were Jewish.

Endless discussions now occurred between my mother and Marysia. What shall we all do next? Marysia was understandably anxious to reunite with her family. She had reestablished contact and knew they were all right. But she wasn't sure that travel was safe yet, and she refused to leave Mama and me alone. She invited us to come home to Przemysl with her, but my mother hesitated to do this.

"Go, Marysia," my mother urged her. "Your husband and children need you. I will manage."

I stopped breathing, waiting for her reply.

"No, not yet," Marysia insisted. "Not until you figure out what to do. Besides," she laughed, "those five hoodlums can take care of themselves."

And I breathed again. Marysia was not leaving.

So both of my mothers stayed, because there was no place else to go. They were earning their keep. Marysia sewed. My mother gave the French lessons and tutored slow learners. And she continued knitting the sweater for hunchbacked, old Mr. Kamienicki. It was nearing completion. Only the sleeves remained to be done. The grandpa chuckled delightedly whenever my mother requested a fitting.

I saw a new side of Mama in these days in Mstow. Whereas in my father's presence she had usually adopted a passive, "feminine" attitude, here she had proved to be strong, resourceful, and independent. I was proud of her.

Discussions about leaving Mstow initially frightened me, but since they led to no immediate action, I allowed myself to relax again. Life continued much the same, except that Russian soldiers now moved into some of the homes, forcing the residents to squeeze into a small part of their already tiny dwellings. The people who took in the Russians did not complain, as everyone was grateful to the liberators. And the soldiers, being used to very little, were not demanding guests. They would get together in the evenings and frequent the local pub. I heard them at night singing noisily in the streets. They often slept during the day, as there was not much for them to do. After a few weeks, the whole contingent moved on.

CHAPTER 11

. . . .

An Unexpected Visitor

Thou hast turned for me
my mourning into dancing . . .
and girded me with gladness.
                    —Psalms 30:11

On Sunday afternoons we often lingered over an early dinner
with the Kamienickis. The adults ate in the dining room,
while we four children crowded around the kitchen counter.
The counter looked out on the village square, where boys and
girls gathered to play.

On one such Sunday, around two months after the war
had ended, twelve-year-old Dora spotted her friends playing
statues. In this game, everyone walks forward in a line, and
when "it" calls "Statues!" they all freeze; whoever fails to

stop instantly is "out." Dora's friends beckoned to her to join them.

"We're all done!" Dora shouted to her parents, though the rest of us were still eating. "We're going out."

"Not so fast," her mother admonished. "Whose turn is it to do the dishes?"

My mother piped up: "Tereska, you stay and help."

We checked the chore list in the kitchen drawer—Dora and I were free today. We happily scooted out the door, while the two younger girls stayed behind with a pout.

By the time we arrived, Dora's friends had changed the game to hide and seek. I was not always included with her friends, but today she was feeling generous.

"Tereska gets to play," she announced, and no one protested. "But you have to be 'it,'" she told me.

The children scattered to find hiding places, while I closed my eyes and started counting to one hundred.

" . . . Ninety-seven, ninety-eight, ninety-nine, one hundred."

* * * * *

I open my eyes. The first thing I see is Marysia, striding toward me across the square. This is surprising, since she takes her meals with a different family and never comes to our house during dinner.

I'm still "it," and I've got to find my hidden playmates. They are waiting for me. But Marysia is waving, and even from a distance I can see an unusually broad smile on her face. Now I notice a man, lagging a few steps behind. There is something about the tilt of his fedora hat, or the way he swings his arms . . . . As the two people get closer, I recognize the man: my father.

We should have been playing statues, because I freeze in mid step. I forget my job as "it" and totally ignore the disgruntled shouts of the hiders. "Hey, Tereska," an angry voice yells. "Get a move on." Another shouts, "Don't you know how to play, stupid?" This voice I recognize as Dora's.

Out of the corner of my eye I see the children jumping out from behind doorways, fences, and trees, regrouping in the little park. Another "it" is counting: " . . . twelve, thirteen, fourteen . . ."

Marysia and my father seem to be floating toward me in slow motion, like disembodied spirits.

I panic. In the relative safety of Mstow, my mother has not drilled me in the details of our current identity. What has she told our hosts? The picture of the SS man in the Przemysl ghetto flashes in my mind. "Is this your mother?" he had asked me about Marysia. If I had given the wrong answer, we would both have been killed. What is the answer now? Has my mother revealed that she has a husband? Am I supposed to have a father? How will we introduce this man? How should I act toward him?

Much in the way he received me when I arrived in Warsaw, I do not run to greet him. Instead, I dash into the house, where my mother and the other adults are still chatting over tea.

"You have a visitor," I say to Mama, breathless, my voice shaking with the effort to calm it.

Tatus and Mama.

"A visitor? Excuse me," she says to the Kamienickis, rising from the table. Slowly rising, everything still happening slowly, in unreal time, slow motion. Until she opens the door and with a shriek springs into his arms, and time whirls fast now as they hug and kiss and cry right there in the street, in the public square, where even the surprised robins chirping in the trees can see.

Marysia watches from a few feet away, and I skirt around the joyful couple to join her, to hold her hand. At some point my father turns to me, admires how I've grown, hugs and kisses me—at some point he does these things, I'm sure, though I don't remember them at all. What I do recall is clinging to Marysia's hand and witnessing my parents' happiness, my mind slipping back to the game of hide and seek still thriving in the square. I'm thinking of rejoining the game. This time someone else can be "it." This time I want to hide.

CHAPTER TWELVE

● ● ● ● ● ● ● ● ● ● ● ● ● ● ● ● ● ● ●

Together Again

Life can only be understood backwards,
but it must be lived forwards.
　　　　　　　—Soren Kierkegaard

Apparently now it was all right to have a father. The
Kamienickis welcomed him inside, joined in the celebration,
broke out a hidden bottle of pre-war vodka and a still
untouched sour-cherry strudel. How did he survive the
Warsaw Uprising? everyone wanted to know. But my father,
exhausted from trekking over miles of muddy roads, just fell
asleep on their couch. My mother pulled off his boots. Mrs.
Kamienicki covered him with her black shawl. Mama sat by
him and watched him breathe.

It wasn't until the next day that he told his story.

When the Uprising started, the Nazis picked him up on the street and herded him into a firing line. He pretended to be blind—which, with his glasses hidden in his pocket, he practically was. Following their twisted "ethical" code, the Nazis chose not to shoot a blind man. Released from the firing line, Tatus stumbled off and tried to concentrate on a possible destination rather than on the shots and screams behind him.

He headed for a small town called Podkowa Lesna, where, someone had told him, the citizens were helping the Polish insurgents. He knocked on a door, said he could not see well enough to fight, and needed shelter. The Pomianowskis, total strangers, let him in. Never revealing his Jewish identity, he stayed with these good people until the end of the war.

"But how did you find us?" my mother asked.

An office in Warsaw informed him that the tiny remnant of Uprising survivors from our area had been sent to three little villages.

"I prayed that you would be in one of them," he said.

I wondered to which God he prayed.

"How did you get here?" I asked. "Did someone drive you?"

"I walked," he answered with a touch of pride. "First I walked to one of the towns, but you were not there. Mstow was my second stop. I asked around if anyone had seen two women and a child from Warsaw . . ." He paused as tears locked his throat.

"Come, Kit-kit," he said to me, abruptly changing the subject. "Climb on the horsey." He stretched out his hands and legs.

This was a game we used to play when I was very small, and despite some reluctance to get back into that role, I went along. I understood that he was trying to reconnect, and I knew that neither of us knew how. So I stepped onto his stocking feet; his boots were still drying on the porch. Holding hands, our arms tautly stretched and our elbows locked, he tried to ride me up and down. But I was much heavier now, and he was weak. His feet were swollen. He couldn't lift me. I slipped off his feet, embarrassed for both of us.

My father's arrival spelled the end of the peaceful interlude in Mstow. The soft straw mattress where I had nestled between my mother and Marysia turned into a scratchy outpost for my parents. Marysia found other lodging so my parents could sleep together. My mother now occupied the middle of the mattress, while I struggled to maintain some space on the edge. Frequently I woke up on the floor.

My parents were celebrating a second honeymoon. I felt alone and left out as they huddled together and whispered in the night.

If they made love, I don't remember noticing. One night, however, a wonderful new sensation stirred in my body, and I found that by squeezing my legs together I could make the feeling intensify. It comforted me when I felt alone. Though no one had ever told me that comforting myself in this way was wrong, I somehow felt guilty, as if I had done something sinful. So while my parents shared their secrets, I suffered alone with mine. I wished my father had never come back.

For a time I was kept in the dark regarding my parents' plans for the future. I eavesdropped intently on their hushed conversations, pretending to be absorbed in knitting the sweater for my teddy bear. But this ruse often failed, since my parents switched to German, which they both spoke fluently, when they suspected that "little pitchers have big ears."

Not long after my father's arrival, however, my parents revealed their plan: very soon we would be leaving Mstow. Of course this made sense—what in the world would my father do in a backward little farm village?—but to me it seemed heartless.

The worst part: Marysia would not join us. She was returning to her family.

Once the decision was made, my mother pushed to start on the road. She ached to leave this place where she had suffered my father's absence—this place where I had learned to play, to feed a goat, to catch a ball.

My father, though equally eager, pointed to the almost completed green sweater for old Mr. Kamienicki. One sleeve still hung on the knitting needles; then the pieces had to be sewn together and the brown buttons that Marysia had donated needed to be attached.

Marysia offered to take over the job, but my father objected.

"You have to finish the sweater yourself," he told Mama. "These people have been good to you and the child. We have our whole lives ahead of us. We can wait another few days."

He rubbed his hands in the way he did when sharing good news.

"As long as we're together, Kit-kit, that's all that counts. Right?" he said, bending down toward me with a big smile. And at that moment I was glad to have my father again.

So the green sweater dictated our departure date. When the grandpa tried on the final product, the whole Kamienicki family marveled at how perfectly it fit.

"I guess you can make a sweater for a hunchback after all," the old man said, strutting around the kitchen. His back seemed straighter than ever before.

The Kamienickis prepared a farewell feast of ham, sauerkraut, and potato pierogi. They laughed as my father told how he used to help his wet-nurse, Kasia, cook pierogi. He pretended to be a little boy, tottering on a wobbly stool, his face screwed up with intensity, his tongue licking his lips as his fingers clumsily glued together the little ears of dough.

By the time we were ready to go, I had come to terms with this latest change in my life. As we waved goodbye to Mstow—and to Marysia—I did not cry. My father had prepared us for an adventure and I was looking ahead.

It certainly did not occur to me that I might never see Marysia again.

*   *   *   *   *

The picture of adventure my father had painted generally lived up to its promise: We will live in a big city, he told me, with parks and stores and cars and trolleys and moviehouses, and we will live in a fine apartment and you will go to a big school and I will have a good job and make lots of money and we will be together and will not have to be afraid. This paradise turned out to be Bydgoszcz, a medium-size industrial city, busier with stores and traffic than any place I had ever seen, even Warsaw. Our apartment faced a noisy main drag, where, indeed, trolleys clanged, trucks honked, and automobiles whizzed by, discharging fumes. Stores had little to sell, but their practically bare windows still attracted the attention of passersby strolling on the sidewalk.

The building into which we moved, five stories high, stood taller than most. The area had not been bombed. Compared to the mountain of rubble that I remembered as Warsaw, Bydgoszcz looked prosperous and pristine. Church spires still stretched toward the sky. Rebuilt statues still watched over ornate public buildings, and marble fountains in the park provided perches for pigeons.

Tatus once took me to the park, where men in bear costumes stopped to talk to children. I was scared by them rather than entertained. I refused to shake hands with a terrifying bear, and the man in the costume had to unzip the furry paw and show his hand to reassure me.

A medical office for my father was right next to our apartment. In addition to seeing private patients, Tatus also got a job, in the hospital, with an old friend's help.

"It is quite an honor to be Director of Pediatrics," my father boasted. He regaled my mother and me with tales of the respect and love both patients and staff showed him.

"The nurses are crazy about me," he would tease Mama. The nurses were nuns.

My father and me in
Bydgoszcz, 1945.

When he saw patients in the home office, my father
insisted on total silence in our apartment, which was separated from the office by a pair of smoked-glass double doors.
Our failure to meet his standard, by even walking across the
creaking floor, led to daily arguments, which escalated in
volume as my parents' new honeymoon period waned.

One time my father grabbed his coat and stormed out of
the apartment. Mama locked herself in the bedroom. Left

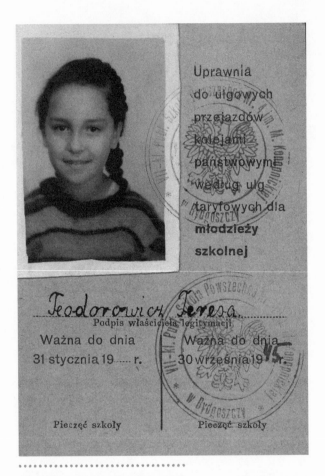

Another false identity, 1945.

alone, I tried to shut out her sobs. I took out the numbered notebook in which I kept my paper dolls. Little Pavelek, the real doll left behind in Lvov, had never been replaced. But paper dolls made excellent substitutes. I was slowly collecting a schoolroomful. So far four dolls lived in my notebook, which I thought of as "The Convent." Each doll had her name and age written on her back, as well as the page in the notebook that was her home. That page held not only the doll but all her clothes. Slipping into the world of make-believe, I tuned out the sounds of now softer whimpering and labored breathing coming from Mama's room.

Instead of playing "convent," the dolls and I now played house. Three dolls were sisters who had fun swimming in a lake that I drew on a separate page. The fourth doll was the mother. There was no father.

The prosperous life in Bydgoszcz came at a price. We had to continue hiding our true identities. My father explained that he would lose his job if the hospital knew that we were Jews. At dinner he would tell us about Jewish professionals who had been fired, and about outbreaks of anti-Semitic violence around the city. The war was over and the Nazis were gone, but we still had to contend with the deep anti-Semitism of many Polish people as well as of the new Communist regime and its Russian backers. We were still in danger.

My parents again changed my name. The false identity papers that my father had used during the war belonged to a Mieczyslaw Teodorowicz, a Pole of Armenian origin. Since we were now reunited as a family, my mother and I took my father's false name. And so I was no longer Irena Stefania Licht, or Teresa Chrystyna Urban, or even Teresa Chrystyna Kaliszewska. I was now Teresa Chrystyna Teodorowicz, a nine-year-old Catholic girl.

Continuing to live as a Catholic was no problem for me. I never even considered any other possibility. I fit right into the third grade. Though always a fairly shy child, I found it easy to make friends. Just as in Mstow, my status as "the new girl" made me a celebrity. Even in the metropolitan center of Bydgoszcz, a new arrival brought with her an air of excitement, curiosity, new possibilities. Girls flocked around me and welcomed me into their midst.

We rarely played in my house, though the girls sometimes invited me to theirs. My parents understandably feared strangers, who might discover more than we wanted them to know. Mostly I saw my friends in school, in church, and at girl scout meetings. Going from one place to another, we linked arms and walked in step.

The rules for belonging differed with location and age. In Mstow, you could be accepted by playing children's games. Here, a more sophisticated group of nine-year-olds focused on the nationalistic pride entailed in being girl scouts, and on the exchange of artistically executed entries in one another's "autograph books."

CHAPTER THIRTEEN

. . . .

Autograph Album

To leave is to die a little.
—French proverb

Scouting had always been a serious undertaking in Poland. My father used to tell how, as a teenager, he became a leader of the Jewish scouts in his town. Before the war, such activities were permitted to Jews. Tatus would describe in minute detail the special uniform he wore and how his Kasia would proudly sew on the badges of distinction he earned over the years.

"We were fervent Zionists," my father used to say. "We were preparing to establish a Jewish state of Palestine and to emigrate there some day." The young scouts considered themselves important pioneers in Zionism, the Jewish struggle for a homeland.

As a new girl scout, how proud I was to be following in my father's footsteps! Though my troop's activities centered on Polish, not Jewish, nationalism, Tatus wholeheartedly supported them. He often bought expensive accessories for my basic uniform—much against Mama's better judgement.

My uniform consisted of a bluish-gray skirt with overblouse to match. A slightly darker scarf was worn around the neck, pulled through a wooden ring at the throat. The cap was a beret with a fleur-de-lis embroidered in front. A shiny rope swung from shoulder to waist. Stripes or patches of distinction decorated the uniforms of deserving scouts and identified the troop. I felt at least six inches taller in this impressive outfit. My mother washed and ironed it before each meeting, and my father inspected my shoes, hair, and nails.

The basic uniform as well as accessories were sold in a special scouting store. Each time my parents took me there, I admired and longed for the belt. It was not required; it was strictly a luxury. It was a wide, substantial, etched leather belt, with a shiny buckle on which an eagle was engraved. Only a few of my peers owned one; most made do with a simple tied rope. So when my father offered to buy the belt for me, I dragged him to the store the very same day.

I inaugurated my prize at the next parade. The scouts marched in nationalistic parades every few weeks, to celebrate one or another Polish victory or to honor Communist holidays. During our troop meetings, we learned to march in straight rows of two abreast, to start, stop, and turn in smart unison. We learned to sing patriotic songs and shout slogans, while our leaders impressed upon us the glory of living—or dying—for our Fatherland. We were the Daughters of the Polish People. Poland's future depended on us.

Marching to the rhythm of the band, usually led by our male counterparts, fixing my eyes on the red and white flags held high by the color guard, I cherished my exalted identity as the daughter of my Fatherland—and of my father.

Tatus fastened the belt buckle that first day out. It pinched my stomach, so I loosened it a bit as the troop leader prepared us for the festivities. During the parade, I frequently sneaked glances down at my belt and stuck my belly out just enough to attract my partner's attention.

"Wow, are you lucky," she obliged me by saying. She despondently fingered the stringy thing tied around her own waist. "My parents would never spend that kind of money."

But when I came home from the parade, eager to share the afternoon's events, my father's frown stopped me. He was looking at my middle and, as my hand jumped to it, I realized that the belt was gone. I couldn't believe it. My whole world shattered. Not only had I lost my hard-won treasure, not only would I suffer the scorn of my troopmates, but I was a total disappointment to my parents.

Mama helped to relieve my guilt by scolding me for always losing things. She was right, I felt. I couldn't be trusted with anything. I wished my father would scold me, too, but as predictably as he yelled at my mother, he rarely showed anger toward me. He dried my tears with his big white handkerchief and then pretended to squeeze rivers of water out of it. When he finally coaxed a smile out of me, he promised to scour the parade route and inquire at all possible scouting

Jewish scouts in Poland, about 1915.
My father is in the front row, right.

locations. We conducted the search together, but the belt was nowhere to be found.

Besides scouting, a major activity among my peers centered around autograph albums. Shortly after my arrival in Bydgoszcz, I noticed the girls (boys went to different schools) passing little books back and forth between them. Inside these, the children wrote and illustrated brief inspirational sayings, slogans, or verses. Every girl's album circulated throughout the class, each girl taking one album home at a time and devoting several days to choosing and meticulously executing her contribution in her finest penmanship. The entries were decorated with colorful flowers or designs. The whole thing was a work of art.

That day it was my mother whom I dragged to a store. I chose a small album, no bigger than my hand, with carved red flowers blooming on its wooden cover. The word Pamietnik stretched in blue letters across the cover. A "book of memories."

"May I be the first to write in your autograph book?" Mama asked.

"Sure," I said, happy to give the little album a start.

In the next few days, she pored over loose pieces of paper, scribbling, scratching out, and starting again.

"I'm working on my message to you," she would say, shooing me away when I tried to peek. "I want it to say exactly what I mean."

Impatient, I urged her to hurry. I wanted to take my album to school. Finally she handed me the little book. Although the first to inscribe it, she chose a page toward the middle. In her beautiful, flowing hand she wrote—in Polish, of course:

When you are grown, Tereska dear,
And through this album chance to peer,
You'll find that yellow now dims the page,
But your mother's heart has not changed with age.
To my beloved little daughter,

Mamusia, Bydgoszcz, October 8, 1945

I hardly noticed what she had written. It was, after all, just my mother.

Ela was my best friend in school, because we sat together in a double desk, and when we lined up I always stood right

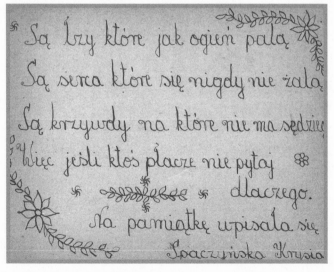

Some samples from my autograph book.

behind her. We lined up by size, the smallest in front, and she was the only child who was shorter than I. For this I loved her. Ela, therefore, was the first with whom I exchanged albums.

I could hardly finish supper, so excited was I to start the inscription. My parents both offered to help. My father suggested verses from the poems of Mickiewicz, something about a bird who loved a rose from Oscar Wilde, a poem or two that he composed himself. My mother looked through my schoolbooks, some of which contained inspirational sayings. I chose a selection from a child's book of verses; the angel on the cover appealed to me.

Under my mother's watchful eye, I practiced drawing lines on scrap paper and writing in my best penmanship, careful not to spill or smear the ink. I practiced several times until I felt confident to transfer the inscription to the real album. My mother helped to draw faint guide lines in pencil and, finally, I ventured my first autograph entry:

To dear Ela,
  The heart of a child
  Is a little church
  In which an angel hides.
  The angel whispers
  You must do good.
  And don't be bad,
  It chides.

> *Remember me,*
> *Your friend,*
> *Teresa Teodorowicz*

Lacking artistic ability, I talked my mother into sketching a colorful bunch of flowers, which I copied into a corner of the page. The whole process took almost a week, by which time Ela was ready with mine. We exchanged albums. I was delighted that she liked my poem. For hers she had chosen a patriotic theme:

If you must suffer, keep up the fight,
For Polish youth all know,
That suffering is their guiding light
God grant it help us grow.

A colorful wreath encircled the verse, and her name appeared at the bottom.

Exchanging autograph albums with everyone in the class took many weeks, and I became totally absorbed in the process. It was fun to see the little book's pages grow fuller and fuller. Even my teacher made an entry:

As life goes on, remember dear,
Wherever you may go,
That each of us is born right here,
A person and a Pole.
This sacred truth above the rest
Must always guide your goal:
In the fervent Polish breast
Lies the loving human soul.

> *To sweet, well-behaved Tereska*
> *With best wishes for a happy future,*
> *Karowska, teacher*
> *Bydgoszcz, November 23, 1945*

• • • • •

November 1945. We had lived in Bydgoszcz for three or four months by then. Marching proudly (even without my belt) in the militaristic parades devoted to praising Poland and the Soviets, watching the autograph-book entries mount, I felt rooted. I belonged here. I even resumed counting consecutive communions, partly because my friends were doing it, and partly, perhaps, because an undercurrent of fear in my family had reawakened thoughts of death. My parents knew that our lives were still in danger, that at some point someone would realize that we were Jews. There seemed to be no reason why I couldn't make it to salvation now. My previous effort, in the convent, had failed due to the Warsaw Uprising. In Mstow, I had not resumed my quest. But now the war was over, and to me the road to a trouble-free, stable future seemed a straight line. Surely I wouldn't be uprooted again.

• • • • •

During this time, most people in Poland were living in terrible conditions, with little food or medicine, few utilities and other services, and the prospect of living in poverty for years to come. In an odd twist of fate, my family—though non-Christian—was enjoying a period of peace and prosperity. My biggest concern was the Christmas play that my class was preparing—my first dramatic opportunity since the ill-fated Mother's Day performance in Przemysl. I was to be an angel, and my mother was sewing a splendid costume. Each day after school I rushed home to see how far the costume had progressed. The frilly white gown, made from a discarded curtain, reminded me of my First Communion dress. I floated around the house in whatever state of completion I found the dress. My mother worried that I would rip the seams or sit on the pins, but I floated carefully. I loved trying on the halo, which my mother had fashioned from wire covered with curtain scraps.

But the best part was the wings. They were cut from a cardboard box in which we had brought our few possessions from Mstow. (Now we were sufficiently well off to buy luggage.) I helped my mother paint them white with a broad brush, and then used a narrow brush to produce gold details. The method of attachment proved a challenge, since the wings weighed too much for a simple string, but finally my mother rigged up strong straps. The wings were to be slipped on like a knapsack. To my great frustration, the wings could never be tried on, because they were either wet or in some sort of fragile state that made them off limits. "Another few days," my mother kept promising. "And don't worry. They'll be ready for Christmas."

A lot can change in a month, though. We hadn't counted on the impact of the arrival of my grandmother, Babcia.

Babcia had moved in with us several weeks earlier. Soon after arriving in Bydgoszcz, my parents had started a search for our relatives. Aunt Berta's family had last been seen in the Przemysl Jewish ghetto, where Marysia had taken me for the life-threatening visit. Through letters to Marysia, my parents quickly discovered that the family was still in

Przemysl. A Christian couple had hidden them when the Germans liquidated the ghetto.

The search for Babcia took longer. We knew that she had remained in Lvov when my parents left for Warsaw. She would not abandon the city where her son—my Uncle Artur—might be looking for her. But had she survived the war? My "brother" Jurek—Marysia's son with the mischievous smile—offered to look for her. Success! My grandmother had been in hiding with a Christian family, though the family that sheltered her had done so in exchange for her remaining diamonds.

It took a lot of pleading on Jurek's part to pry Babcia away from Lvov, where she was still waiting for Artur. Jurek finally convinced her that, if Artur were alive, he would find us in Bydgoszcz. Registries of survivors searching for relatives were kept in central locations. Besides, wouldn't Uncle Artur check with Marysia?

Babcia, looking grayer and more wrinkled than I remembered her, sighing a lot and often breaking into tears, finally arrived in Bydgoszcz with Jurek. He still sported the crooked smile, and the funny faces that he made lifted the chronic aura of tension that overlaid daily life in our house. Between the strains of living with my father's unpredictable temper and the stress of continuing to hide who we were, our family was rarely relaxed. I recalled my life with Marysia and the four brothers and secretly wanted Jurek to take me back with him to Przemysl.

Babcia moved in, not only into my bedroom, but into my bed. She complained about my kicking her at night. She objected to the way my father treated my mother.

The family arguments now grew into a triangle. As for me, I could no longer lay my paper dolls out on the bed before going to sleep. I began playing in the dark, pretending that my fingers were the dolls.

Babcia contributed an unmistakable air of gloom to our already tense household. Despite the daily marital battles, gloom had not marked our family before. When not angry, my father was upbeat, optimistic, playful. My mother's temperament was generally placid. But Babcia was waiting for her son Artur. She kept constant vigil. Would he really find her here, miles from Lvov? she would ask my mother a hundred times a day.

The last she had heard from him was in the middle of the war. He had written from Janowska concentration camp, on little scraps of surreptitiously acquired paper, begging for money to buy his way out of imminent death. He described growing hunger, disease, and terror, and sneaked the notes out through some sort of underground network. One of the letters he sent to Babcia read:

Dear Mama,
I got your last letter, for which I thank you.
Don't be surprised that I am in such a pessimistic frame of mind but it's not surprising, since I am not anticipating anything happy in the coming days. I have maximum several days' time. I received the money, 200zl, but that's nothing. Even if I could arrange something, I wouldn't have a penny. Here every step costs thousands.

I have already lost hope.
Kisses and regards, Tusiek [Artur]

Babcia had sent him the money, selling her four-carat diamond ring, a diamond-studded silver butterfly pin, and several heavy gold necklaces and bracelets. She had entrusted the cash to the messenger who brought her the notes, a young Pole who claimed to have bribed some German guards.

The money never got to my uncle, though Babcia sent more several times. The messenger insisted that he had delivered it personally to an intermediary contact person. Babcia didn't trust him, but he was her only hope.

Artur's notes became increasingly more desperate. And then they stopped altogether.

And so, although months had passed since the end of the war and many survivors had already located the remnants of their loved ones, Babcia refused to believe that her son could be dead. Surely he would call or walk in the door at any minute. With each dawn came new hope. With each ring of the telephone came an intake of breath, a pleading look in her eyes.

"Who is it?" Babcia would interrupt my father as he spoke with an unidentified caller. He would give her an irritated look and later would yell at her.

"Don't you think I would tell you if it was Artur? Do you take me for a total fool?"

With each doorbell, a frantic rush to the door. Just a patient for my father. And then the tears.

My heart broke each time the inevitable disappointment

hit. I expressed my discomfort by becoming short and irritable with Babcia.

My parents were also showing the strain. In my father's view, Babcia's presence endangered our lives. She did not know how to play the game; during the war Babcia had remained hidden and never had to use her assumed name. She also spoke Polish with a pronounced Jewish accent, guttural *r*'s, deep throated *ch*'s—and with Yiddish expressions frequently thrown in, like *nu*, a long, drawn-out equivalent of "so-o-o." Consequently, my parents kept her under house arrest, so to speak. But she did need to go out once in a while.

There was the time she went to the dentist.

"What is your name?" the dentist asked. A reasonable question. But Babcia could not remember her assumed name. Shaken, she returned home and reported what happened.

My father proceeded to have a tantrum more memorable than most. "You will send me to my grave," he threatened, holding his heart.

I was terrified that he would die, but also furious at him. "Stop yelling at Babcia," I said to myself, under my breath. "How could she help it? It's not her fault!" Anger was beginning to replace my fear of him.

The next incident broke the proverbial camel's back. I blamed myself for this one, though no one had accused me.

Mrs. Pomianowska, the Catholic friend who had sheltered my father during the Warsaw Uprising, was spending a few days with us. A kind, gracious woman, she did not know—or at least, admit to knowing—that we were Jewish.

• • • • •

One day both of my parents go out in the morning, leaving me and Babcia with Mrs. Pomianowska. I get ready for school, and Babcia packs my lunch. Finally I grab my books and lunchbox, and scoot down the stairs.

The street is humming with traffic, and I wait for a trolley to clatter by. Soon a truck blocks my view of it. I look both ways, again spotting the trolley with passengers dangling from its sides, now disappearing into the distance. The coast seems clear. I start to cross the street right in front of my house. I do this every day, but perhaps today I have been distracted by the trolley. The next thing I know, I am lying under a truck. I'm on my back, staring at the metal underside of the vehicle, which looms just inches away from my nose. Luckily, the giant wheels straddle my body.

Terrified, I momentarily lose consciousness. When I come to, I am sprawled in a stranger's arms. He is carrying me. Out of the corner of my eye I notice my schoolbooks scattered on the sidewalk. We enter my building. Still woozy, I hear him ask, "Is this your house?" Apparently he found the address on my notebooks. I utter a weak "Yes."

In the front lobby, the man finds the appropriate doorbell and presses it urgently. He pushes it repeatedly and I hear the ringing upstairs, once, twice, three times. It frightens me more than being run over by the truck. It reminds me of the Nazis bursting into our home in Lvov. I want to tell the man to stop, but the words stick in my mouth. He keeps leaning on the bell. Suddenly Babcia appears, peering over the banister. She sees me stretched out like a sack of potatoes draped over a stranger's arms.

"*Oy, veys mir!*" Babcia screams her alarm in Yiddish. "*Oy, mein Gottiniu!*" She thinks I am dead.

She races down the stairs, Mrs. Pomianowska close behind.

Even half-unconscious, I realize that Babcia's Yiddish outburst spells trouble.

•　•　•　•　•

While I suffered only a few bruises on the arm and leg nearest to a wheel, Babcia had to endure my father's wrath. How he found out what she had screamed on those stairs, I'll never know. According to my parents, Mrs. Pomianowska didn't say a word. Perhaps she had known all along that we were Jews. In any case, she would not have given us away. Still, it was our final warning, as I would soon find out.

•　•　•　•　•

The Christmas play is only days away. I come home from school and see my wings resting majestically on the living-room couch. They are ready, except for the straps needed to sling them over my shoulders. I run to admire them.

"Can I try on the whole costume?" I ask. "Mama, you can hold up the wings while I look in the mirror."

I head for the closet where the rest of the angel costume hangs.

"Not now," my mother says, pulling up a chair close to hers. "Come join us here. We have something to tell you." My parents are leafing through piles of official-looking papers strewn around the dining-room table. Their faces are taut with tension, a different kind of tension from that caused by an argument. My stomach starts to ache.

"What . . . ?"

"We are leaving Poland," my mother replies.

"When?" I'm used to the unexpected.

"Tonight, at midnight."

I hear a sigh from the bedroom, where Babcia sits slumped with her head in her hands.

"Artur," she whispers when I catch her eye. "He will never find me."

"Aunt Berta and her family are coming with us," Tatus says before I have a chance to react. His words tumble over each other with great speed. I can see that he is nervous. Nevertheless, he rubs his hands and grins in that wide-eyed little-boy way he does when about to impart good news. "Isn't that wonderful?"

At the prospect of seeing Aunt Berta, a tickle of joy competes with the pain in my stomach. Our last contact had been in the Przemysl ghetto.

But suddenly the whole thing hits me. We are leaving again. The count of successive communions will again be broken—and somehow I sense that this had been my last chance. Then there is the Christmas play. I break into tears.

"What about my wings?" I cry. "Can we take them with us?"

"No, dear," Mama says. "We can take very little."

My father continues to paint a rosy picture.

"We'll be going on a big truck, in the middle of the

night," he says to me. "You will get to sit in the back, just like the haywagon you used to love in Mstow. It will be fun. Something to remember."

What I remember is the feel of bodies and the smell of sweat in the crowded truck jostling us out of Warsaw. I recall the warmth of Mama's and Marysia's bodies and the rough feel of the winter coat from the convent. I almost start laughing, as the stork's nest jumps into my mental view, and I now—sort of—get the jokes.

My father is explaining the process. We are going to use yet another set of false identity papers. This time we are Armenians returning to our native country.

I don't ask for explanations. My father tends to be long-winded, and I have gotten into the habit of tuning him out. Anyway, no explanation would make sense. Why are we now Armenians? Nothing makes sense. I assume that my parents understand, and I simply go along.

● ● ● ● ●

Later I learned that the Communist government in control of Poland had closed emigration. No Poles (never mind Jews!) could leave the country. Foreign nationals, however, especially those with connections to the Soviet Union, were allowed to return to their lands. So my father's Armenian papers were coming in very handy. Still, despite the protection of our false papers, clear passage was not assured. We had to cross the border illegally, an act called "crossing the green border." It involved bribing border officials, who would stamp the papers and collect their fee.

"The important thing," Tatus was saying when I tuned back in, "is that since we don't speak Armenian, we can't say a word at the border crossing. The driver will do all the talking. Understand?"

Yes, I understand. Silence has become second nature to me.

As my father continues, I am thinking about what I will take, what I can take. I finger the medallion of the Virgin Mary, still hanging around my neck. I must remember that. And the tiny teddy bear from the children in Mstow. And my *pamietnik*, the autograph album, my priceless little book of memories.

Pamietnik! Krysia Spaczynska has it. It was her turn to write in it, and I had just given it to her in class last week.

"Krysia has my *pamietnik*," I choke out. "I can't go without it."

"Oh, what a shame," Mama says, folding an arm around me, stroking my hair. She had helped with at least twenty of my friends' entries, read all of those in my book, and had worked so hard on her own. She knows how much it means. "But unfortunately . . ."

"Where does Krysia live?" my father interrupts, jumping out of his chair, as if with sudden inspiration.

I tell him.

"When we finish packing, we will go and get your book."

"Are you crazy?" Babcia exclaims. She has now joined us at the table. " We are leaving the country tonight! Besides, the snow is a mile high."

As usual, my father ignores her.

At nine o'clock in the evening we ring the doorbell at Krysia's house.

"So sorry to disturb you at this hour," my father apologizes to Mrs. Spaczynska, "but we're going away for the holidays and Tereska would like to take along her *pamietnik*."

"Krysia!" the mother calls, with an edge of annoyance, getting her daughter out of bed. She reluctantly invites us in, and we brush the snow from our coats. Sleepy-eyed, my friend trudges out in pink pajamas, carrying the little album.

"Read what I wrote," Krysia insists, wanting to show off. While Mrs. Spaczynska impatiently taps her foot, I find the page in the album and read Krysia's entry:

There are tears that burn like fire,
There are hearts that suffer and tire,
That are wrongs which no judge can try,
So when someone is crying, don't ask him why.

Remember me,
Your friend, Krysia Spaczynska
Bydgoszcz, 18. XII. 1945

I clutch my treasure on the way home, walking for the last time through the dark streets of Poland. Tatus holds my free hand. He is quiet now, and all I hear is the snow crunching under our feet. When I look up at him, his eyes are focused in the distance. I sense that he is worried, preoccupied. Armenians, green borders, midnight escapes. It all sounds dangerous, and he is the captain of the ship. My mother and I, Babcia and Aunt Berta's family are all depending on him, trusting him. And yet, only three hours before departure, this man, my father, took the time to rescue a little girl's memories.

CHAPTER FOURTEEN

Vienna, City of Dreams

Oh what I would give
If I could relive
Those days in Vienna again...
—popular song

We returned with the autograph book to find my mother and Babcia stuffing things into burlap sacks. My angel wings had been tossed into a corner of the living room, along with a couple of my school notebooks. I picked up the wings and had started to dust them when the doorbell rang.

I stopped in my tracks. Who could be coming to our house now, at night, when we were getting ready to leave? My heart beat faster as fear sank into my belly. I looked at my father for information on what this could mean; but he was already heading for the door, and I could see that he was smiling.

The door opens and four people, their coats sprinkled with snow, burst into the room. I drop the wings and run into the arms of my cousin Olga!

Aunt Berta, Uncle Marek, and my two cousins are standing right there as big as life. A shadow of that frightening night in the Przemysl ghetto, when a Nazi guard stopped Marysia and me, flickers briefly in my mind. But joy chases it away. Hugs and kisses fly all around, and my father and Aunt Berta cling to each other like lovers in the movies. Tears are flowing down their faces so much that I feel embarrassed. They haven't seen each other since the war began, six years ago. I end up clutching Olga and won't let go no matter how much she tickles me in every rib I own. What an evening! First I get my autograph book back, and now this. Who cares about the Christmas play!

As my father had promised, Aunt Berta and her family will be leaving Poland with us. I'm delighted.

"What is my name now that we are Armenians?" I ask, and the grownups smile.

No new name, it seems. All I have to remember—they insist on reminding me—is to keep totally still when we cross the border. After all, none of us knows a single word of Armenian! So if any guard comes into the truck to inspect, we'll just pretend that we're fast asleep.

Taking advantage of the grownups' good mood, I venture another question:

"Where are we going?"

But everyone is already bustling about, packing whatever

can still fit into the sacks, a million conversations going on at the same time. I tug on Olga's skirt.

"Do you know where we are going?" I ask.

Olga always has time for me.

"Vienna," she says, giving me a hug. "Do you remember our cousin Jozek Licht and his wife, Ala?"

I vaguely recall a short, bald man with an elegant woman who smelled of cologne. They used to visit us long ago, in Katowice, before the war.

"They owned a beautiful apartment in Vienna. It was taken over by the Nazis," Olga explains. But when the Americans occupied Vienna and threw the Nazis out, they gave the property back to our cousins. We will be staying with them for a while.

• • • • •

Vienna. The word was magic. Besides his wet-nurse, Kasia, Vienna was my father's favorite subject for stories. He had studied at the University of Vienna School of Medicine and made the city sound like a fairyland. He described the opera and the sidewalk cafés and the students who sat and talked for hours and hours about important new developments like Psychoanalysis and Zionism. Music filled every corner. Strolling musicians, playing the violin or accordion or harmonica, would follow you down the street, and Strauss waltzes flowed from the cafés. The opera was the best. My father, just a poor student then, had to save his pennies for school and travel back to Poland to visit his parents and Kasia. But he always scraped up enough for standing room at the Opera House, or perhaps a seat in the back row of the last balcony.

Though my father got to the opera, he had to skimp on the magnificent Viennese pastries. Bake shops overflowed with creamy napoleons and éclairs filled with custard and topped with gobs of whipped cream, juicy plum cake, plump apfelkuchen, crisp butterkuchen, spicy lebkuchen gleaming with sugar sprinkles, and spitzkuchen shaped like a tent. And colorful marzipan fruits, the kind that studded Hansel and Gretel's gingerbread house in the woods.

"I'd press my nose against the bakery windows and enjoy watching other people eat," my father said in a wistful tone of voice.

(Sometimes, in these past few months since the end of the war, my father would hum a tune from Fledermaus, or the Student Prince, perhaps, and ask my mother if she recognized it. Often she did, and then he might invite her to a waltz and they would sing and twirl around the living room. Those were sweet moments, when they danced and did not fight, and they looked into each other's eyes in a way that brought tears to mine.)

• • • • •

"Will we have enough money to buy cakes?" I ask Olga, hoping so much that we will. I want that as much for my father as for myself.

She just laughs and gives me another hug.

But now the doorbell rings again, and this time it's the truck driver who is taking us out of Poland. Last-minute fastening of our sacks takes place.

"You are not taking that stupid down comforter," my father yells at Babcia. "There is no room for it."

"I am," she insists. "I am entitled to two bags. This is what I choose to put in one of them."

"The war is over," he says. "You will find another comforter someplace in this world."

"Not like this one," Babcia maintains. Sometimes she can be pretty stubborn, and the comforter gets thrown onto the waiting truck, along with the other sacks.

Once we are in the truck, we huddle under rough blankets, protected from the snow by a heavy tarp that smells of gasoline. The adults whisper occasionally.

"How much did we pay the driver?" someone asks.

"What did it cost to bribe the border guard?"

"Three border guards, you mean."

I hear these conversations at the edge of my consciousness. They mean nothing to me. Propped between bodies and our sacks of belongings, I take my mind again to the bakeshops of Vienna.

Engrossed in these thoughts, I am startled when the truck grinds to a stop. We have arrived at the border between Poland and Czechoslovakia. We need to pass through Czechoslovakia on the way to Austria. The tension under the blankets heightens. The bodies around me stiffen. I keep as quiet as I can. So do the others. I can hardly hear anyone breathe.

We wait, wondering if the guards will come to check. What if they make us turn back? In some ways, I wish they would. Vienna, for all its glamour, suddenly looms cold. I already feel homesick. But I know that the grownups want to leave Poland, so I force myself to want that, too.

Nobody comes to check under the tarp. We hear voices at the border booth, but within moments we are off again. We are safely out of Poland. The worst is over. The crossing into Austria will not be a problem. My parents sound happy, though it's too dark for me to see their faces. Aunt Berta sticks her head out of the tarp and spits behind her.

"Good riddance to Poland. May we never see it again," she says, pulling her head, already snow-covered, back in.

We all begin to chatter now, starting with whispers, because we are still used to silence, but then we talk louder and louder. Babcia unties her sack and pulls out the massive down comforter.

"See?" she says triumphantly, looking at my father. "The child is cold."

This despite no such sign from me, although it is, in fact, pretty chilly. Babcia emits a sigh of satisfaction and stretches the throw over me. Snug under it, with my head comfortably cradled in Olga's lap, I listen to the snow pelting the tarp. As I drift off to sleep, I can almost taste the sweet cakes in the bakeries of the "City of Dreams."

* * * * *

Vienna failed miserably to live up to its reputation. The war had dimmed its glow. Although not entirely destroyed like Warsaw, the Austrian capital wore severe scars. Seven months after the war, rubble still littered the streets. Bombed-out ruins still gaped between buildings, like so many missing teeth. The Opera House was whole, but the inside looked drab. I could not picture my father spending his last pennies to climb to its highest balcony. Worst of all, the bakeries boasted few pastries. Many shop windows were empty.

Our Viennese cousins, however, proved to be fine hosts. Jozek, balder than I remembered, and his wife, a bit thinner but still elegant, installed us in two extra rooms of the spacious apartment reclaimed from the Nazis. The big rooms, long corridors, and high ceilings absorbed the eight of us without much trouble, along with our sixteen sacks. Our cousins invited us to stay as long as we liked.

We celebrated the New Year of 1946 with dancing to Strauss waltzes coaxed out of a scratchy Victrola. At midnight I proudly sneezed while downing my first thimbleful of champagne.

●　●　●　●　●

The following Sunday, I scoot out of bed and search through my sack for the most presentable outfit I can find.

"Dressed so early?" asks our hostess, still in a bathrobe. The family is gathering around the breakfast table.

"It's Sunday," I say. "I'm ready for church."

Aunt Berta, who has just walked in, stretches out her arms toward me.

"My poor darling," she croons, "you don't have to go to church anymore. You are a Jewish child now!"

Her face crinkles into an expression somewhere between shock and pity. Stunned, I retreat from the table, away from my beloved aunt's beckoning arms. At this moment I hate her. I look around the table. Nobody else speaks. Not even Olga.

I rush out of the dining room and lock myself in the bathroom. I want to hide. I understand my aunt's point. The war is over. Poland is behind us. We don't have to pretend anymore.

But for me, the make-believe has become real. I have been baptized. I am a Catholic. What will I do if they stop me from going to church?

There is a knock on the bathroom door. Annoyed, I figure that someone needs to use the toilet. I open the door reluctantly. There stands my father with a big smile.

"Come on, Kit-kit," he says. "Eat your breakfast. You and I will go to church."

We walk to church together, trodding the fairy-tale streets of my father's Vienna. This used to be such and so, and this was that, he explains as we pass various sights. I hardly hear him, so anxious am I lest we don't find a church. But we do. And when the time comes, I leave my father in the pew and go to the altar for communion. Suddenly I turn back and slide in next to my father.

"I can't take communion," I whisper. "I haven't made confession."

"It's all right," my father assures me. "God will understand."

I slide out again and join the line forming at the altar.

The priest's fingers dip into a silver chalice. He gently places a small white wafer on my tongue. As it slowly dissolves in my mouth, tears trickle down my cheeks. I am doomed. I know that I will never earn salvation. This could be my last communion. I am a Jewish child.

CHAPTER FIFTEEN

. . . .

Refugee Camp

people scattered
the leaves too scattered
and spread...
　　—Kobayashi Issa

Only two weeks after opening our sacks, we were fastening them again. With the help of our Viennese cousins, yet another set of false papers had materialized. These identified us as concentration-camp survivors. A picture of me taken on an outing in Bydgoszcz was attached to a document certifying me as a former inmate of Plaschow concentration-camp. The name under the picture: Theresa Licht. I had regained my original last name.

Apparently these documents assured us of speedy settlement in a Displaced Persons' Camp. The DP, or "refugee," camps had been set up in many places in Europe by UNRRA, the United Nations Relief and Rehabilitation Agency. They were to serve as way-stations to more permanent destinations in other lands. Our final destination, I was told, would be Palestine. Meanwhile, an UNRRA truck driven by a handsome American soldier came to deliver us to a refugee camp called Neu Freiman.

Neu Freiman did not look anything like a camp, certainly not like the terrifying reports of concentration camps that had slowly been trickling in. Neu Freiman was a neatly kept, small German town on the outskirts of Munich. The German residents had been evicted by the Allies, and their homes had been allocated to refugees like us. My parents said that the owners must have been resettled elsewhere. But Babcia, who always voiced what the rest of us were only thinking, hoped they had all been shot.

The UNRRA truck pulled up to a cozy, river-green ranch house with white shutters. A porch with two rocking chairs seemed to be waiting just for me, and I hopped into one immediately. This was a luxury I had always dreamed about.

The adults dragged our sacks inside with the help of the handsome American driver, who turned out to be a Mr. Wachtel, the director of the camp. I followed them in and ran from room to room, amazed that so many rooms could exist in one dwelling. I had never lived in a house before—always in apartments, attics, dormitories, basements, or somebody's floor. Here there were a kitchen, dining room, living room,

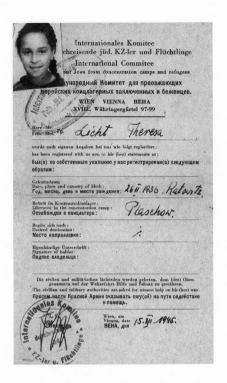

My last fake identity card, this time to gain admittance to a DP camp.

and four bedrooms. The grownups began discussing who would be sleeping where and with whom. I crossed my fingers that I would share my bed with my cousin Olga, but she chose to bunk with her sister, and I ended up with Babcia.

Although my bedroom was the smallest, it had the advantage of a well-placed window. The house stood at the edge of the town, and a chain-link fence marked the boundary between our yard and the world outside the camp. My window looked out on a stretch of uninhabited grassy hills, where, to my great fascination, American soldiers, both black and white, frolicked in the grass with giggling German frauleins.

I had never seen black people before, and was very curious what it would be like to laugh and tumble with them in the grass. Sometimes the soldiers would stop by our fence and throw us boxes of Chicklets chewing gum. Watching me chew, Babcia was amazed to discover that the constant mouth movements that she had observed around here were not some sort of a strange tick. She herself tried chewing only once; the brief pleasure cost her an hour of denture scraping.

I was almost ten by now, and beginning to wonder about things like giggling girls and the men they were with. My curiosity was further piqued by my two cousins, ages nineteen and twenty-one, who whispered a lot at night in the room next to mine.

The two rooms were joined by a door, which was always at least partly cracked, since Babcia refused to close it. Totally disregarding my cousins' pleas for privacy, Babcia insisted that our room was stuffy and a person couldn't breathe. It was stuffy, for sure, because Babcia insisted on covering us with that old down comforter in addition to making me wear wool underpants to bed. Babcia maintained that the most important thing for your health is to keep your bottom warm, and the comforter by itself wouldn't do it, as it was the middle of the winter. So I could hear the content of my cousins' whispers if I listened intently.

It all sounded very mysterious. Sometimes Fela would giggle just like the German girls in the grass; that would be on nights when she had tiptoed home after everyone else was asleep. I'd hear her laughing at the door when she was saying goodnight to this scrawny Romanian Jew with pimples and poor posture.

Actually, all of us refugees were scrawny, with poor posture—and a few missing teeth as well. We also came from many countries, like Poland, Czechoslovakia, Russia, Hungary, Romania, Germany, and Yugoslavia, so everybody spoke a different language. One thing I knew about my cousin Fela was she didn't speak Romanian. I wondered how she understood his jokes enough to find them funny.

I'd have been even more in the dark if it hadn't been for Musia. She was ten, and she lived with her father, grandmother, and a few other relatives in the pale blue house right across the street. Musia had a porcupine in her yard, which is how we met. She wanted to show off her porcupine and how it perked up its quills to ward off danger, but the porcupine didn't think we classified as danger. It just snoozed comfortably even as we blew hard into its off-guard quills. So I kept going across the street every day, and by the time we finally got the porcupine to wake up, Musia and I had become good friends. After that I would spend most of every day at her house, because there was a lot less yelling there, and nobody seemed to be nervous, like my father, or impatient to get to the bathroom. If they had their spats, I never noticed. It wasn't my family, so I didn't care.

Musia was my very first real best friend, the kind that young girls trade secrets with and run to see every chance they get. But I didn't know any good secrets then, and it was a wonder Musia stooped to play with me at all. The only secret I had was that I said my Catholic prayers in bed at night, although I had to say them silently because Babcia and Aunt Berta would kill me if they knew. I was a Jewish child after all, they would say, thank God.

Musia's secrets were a lot more exciting. Her aunt had been a midwife in Russia and delivered babies right in the house, where Musia could observe all the strange goings-on just by pushing the door open a bit. The things she saw through the crack in the door were nothing the nuns had taught us in the convent. Once I repeated some of the information I got from Musia, and Babcia said I shouldn't go to play there anymore.

Babcia was always ready to spoil things, like the time she got rid of a cat that had adopted me. The cat was gone when I came home from school, and Babcia said that he ran away. But Aunt Berta just glared at her, and I knew right there and then that the cat hadn't run away. I hated Babcia for that, but I couldn't hate her for too long, because we shared the same bed and she didn't complain much when I wiggled and kicked her at night. And I couldn't hate her because she cried every day, waiting for Uncle Artur to come knocking on the door.

Anyway, her ideas about me not playing with Musia just evaporated and fortunately, my parents were too busy to ever listen to what Babcia had to say, or to listen to my questions, for that matter. So I continued learning things across the street and stopped asking silly questions at home.

I loved my cousins, especially the older one, Olga. She was short, not much taller than I, not fat, but round and soft. She liked to cook and made amazing things out of flour and potatoes, which we could get in Neu Freiman. Her pierogi may have been the only food to get around my poor appetite. I could finish whole bowlfuls of them. My father compared them favorably to Kasia's pierogi, which was about as high a compliment as one can get. Olga didn't go out with pimply Romanians, and she liked to play with me whenever I felt like it, which was whenever Musia was being punished and kept indoors—Musia's family might not have argued as much as mine, but they were forever punishing her for nothing at all.

When Olga and I were together, we would roll on the bed and wrestle and hug and kiss. Once her sister, Fela, who was checking out her new lipstick in the mirror, saw us touching tongue tips. She yelled at Olga, and Olga said, "Oh come on, she is only a child." I didn't get why you had to be "only a child" just to play tongue touching with your cousin. Plus I didn't think I was a child anymore anyway, and I determined that when I got to be a grownup, I would never consider a ten-year-old person a child.

Both Olga and Fela taught in the Neu Freiman school. It was a pretty strange school. People spoke so many different languages that the administrators decided to hold classes in a language nobody knew: Hebrew. They explained that Hebrew was the modern Jewish language, the language spoken in Palestine. It was the language of the proud, modern Jew, the Jew building a new land, the Jew prepared to fight for his rights. They said Hebrew wasn't like Yiddish, which a lot of the refugees spoke, and with which the Jews "walked into the ovens."

Learning the language of Palestine made sense to me, because my family said we would be going there just as soon as the British would let us in. So we all got Hebrew names, and there I went, changing my name again, this time to Tirtza, which had a bold, almost-teenage ring to it. But I was only called that at school.

At home I continued to be Teresa, or Tereska. Of course, now that we were free, I didn't have to be Teresa anymore; I could go back to Irena. Nobody asked my opinion, though, and my father, whose Jewish soul was heavily peppered with Kasia's Catholicism, believed that St. Teresa had saved my life. And so I remained Teresa, which was fine with me, because I was quite attached to my patron saint, too. She was the perfect saint for me, being still a child when she became a nun and calling herself a little flower of Jesus. In fact, I prayed to her every night along with the usual Our Father's, Hail Mary's, and I Believe's that I whispered without making a sound.

My parents did make some changes in my name, and so now I was Teresa Irena Licht, the Licht being my original last name, while my original first name was now transformed into my middle name. This may all sound confusing, but it was perfectly clear to me, or to anyone who changes names as often as socks.

My cousins didn't have to worry about Hebrew, because they taught art and music. They had never studied to be teachers, but Neu Freiman was not in a position to demand teaching degrees. In February, about a month after our arrival, they decided to put on a Purim play. Every girl in the

Cast of the Purim play, February 1945. I am Queen Esther, front row center.

school wanted to be Queen Esther, but my cousins were in charge, and Olga insisted I get the part. It would be my birthday present. I had just turned ten.

I was delighted. Still mourning the angel wings I had had to leave behind, unused, in Bydgoszcz, I saw this as a new opportunity to shine on the stage. In my exalted role, I would have to sing and dance, both solo. The song would be easy, since carrying a tune was not a requirement, but everyone knew I had two left feet. Fela pointed out this obvious fact to Olga, but Olga had made up her mind.

The dance simply involved sliding sideways across the stage three times and then twirling three times in place. Olga was convinced that I was capable of this. With the weight of her trust upon me, I twirled and tromped correctly, if not gracefully, across the stage during rehearsals, and Olga felt her faith in me to be entirely vindicated.

The actual performance, however, was a disaster. Clad in a regal gown made of a pinned-together lace curtain, I concentrated so hard on the steps that I stumbled on the dragging hem and lost my count in the dance pattern. Suddenly, I found to my horror that I was traversing the stage for the fourth time. How would I ever fit in the twirls? Fela, at the piano, quickly improvised a few extra bars, and so I and the music managed to end at the same time. I was, however, ashamed to come home that day, and no amount of praise and reassurance from both my cousins could erase the feeling that I had let them down.

Some of the DP camps in Europe were terrible places to be, but life in Neu Freiman was easy, especially compared to what had occurred before. UNRRA was taking good care of us. Mr. Wachtel, the American director, frequently stopped by to visit, bearing gifts of chewing gum and cigarettes and offering us rides to the warehouse. I loved going along on these excursions, even if Fela always ended up sitting in the front seat with Mr. Wachtel. We would come home loaded with stuff. The warehouse stocked food and clothing and we would just pick up whatever we needed, for free. Eating the food, though, was another story. The warehouse featured such goodies as powdered eggs, powdered Carnation milk, and Spam. The only way I would eat any of it was in the form of Olga's pierogi. But she didn't make those every day.

Babcia figured it was either my failure to eat ("She's getting thinner every day") or resistance to woolen underwear that brought on the attacks of tonsillitis. Actually I'd fought these since my earliest years, but you can't have surgery when you are running—or hiding—for your life, so my tonsils never came out. Now, my father decided, was the propitious moment. Neu Freiman was near the city of Munich. My father located a doctor there.

•   •   •   •   •

I'm skipping alongside my father on the way to the bus that will take us to the doctor. I'm thrilled to be having my tonsils out. First of all, I'll be spending a few days in the hospital in a room with other children. It will be like a sleepover party. When you're an only child living with a bunch of bickering adults, a few days playing with kids can sound wonderful. I'll be romping around on my very own bed, maybe even pulling someone's hair, like I did in the convent with Koziol. Best of all, as everyone knows, after having your tonsils out, you get unlimited mountains of ice cream.

We arrive in Munich, which has been damaged in the war even worse than Vienna, though not nearly as bad as Warsaw. The doctor's office is on the third floor of a partially bombed-out building. The doctor is an old man, even older than my father, and speaks only German in the rough, guttural growls of the Nazis. His hands are thick and red. And he doesn't even wear a white coat, like my father did when he was practicing medicine. I've been told that I will get an anesthetic and won't feel a thing, so I climb confidently into my father's lap, which is where the doctor tells me to sit.

I've never had an operation before, so I don't object when he tells me to open my mouth and comes at me with a pair of giant gleaming pliers. He plunges into my throat, no anesthesia, and chops off one of my tonsils. I let out a shriek and jump off my father's lap, and he can't stop me even though he is holding my arms. My father and the doctor argue and finally my father explains that the doctor will give me an anesthetic after all, even if they are hard to get and expensive so soon after the war. Before I have time to protest, I'm back in my father's lap and have a mask over my face with something that smells awful and is called ether. I fall asleep and dream of being whirled by my throat on a merry-go-round.

When I wake up, I don't want to play with children in a hospital, and I don't want ice cream. My throat hurts, and I am groggy from the ether. I just want to go home, which is what we do. My cousin Olga sits by my bed and makes up funny stories about characters like "Inga von Binga" and "Roffeldorf von Hoffeldorf," and we don't touch tongues because my mouth hurts too much to open it. We just touch noses, which, Olga says, is how the Eskimos kiss.

●　●　●　●　●

The trauma of the tonsillectomy paled in comparison to what came next. Five months into our mostly idyllic interlude in

Neu Freiman, we received an affidavit from Babcia's cousin in America, inviting us to come to the States. An affidavit guarantees that the host will take care of the guests until they can take care of themselves.

The invitation included Aunt Berta's part of the family, but my Uncle Marek would not hear of it. He had been waiting all his life to get to the "Promised Land," and he wasn't about to change his course now that Palestine was in sight. He was prepared to wait as long as necessary to see his dream come true. My parents were not as idealistic. Who knows if the British will ever let us into Palestine, they said. And here was the opportunity to emigrate to America: a bird in the hand.

CHAPTER 16

"Gott Sei Dank!"

Split at the root,
Neither Gentile nor Jew,
Yankee nor Rebel...
—Adrienne Rich

What in the world was America? During the Warsaw Uprising, I had imagined it as a small, safe room, with a few men quietly smoking pipes. But the image had faded over time and left a blank space.

I felt betrayed. How could I say goodbye to vibrant Aunt Berta and gentle Uncle Marek? To beautiful Fela? To my dearest Olga? How could our two families, just barely reunited, split apart now? I had believed that we would always be together someday, perhaps in Palestine. "As long as we're together," my father had said so many times these past few months, smiling with pride at our reunited circle. "Just as long as we're together." Aunt Berta would smile whenever he said that, and would grasp whoever was nearby in a hearty hug.

And now they were ready to fly to opposite ends of the universe! Could I ever trust adults again?

The only bright gleam in the darkness was that my friend Musia was going to America, too. We would be sailing on the same ship, headed for a city called "Neff York." Although we would share the adventure, Musia could not share my pain. Her whole family was coming. She wasn't leaving her heart behind.

Dreams of other departures began to torture me. Leaving my parents, leaving Marysia, leaving Mstow, leaving my angel wings. One night I dreamt about the furtive tromp through snowy Bydgoszcz to reclaim my autograph book. I woke up in a panic. Where was my autograph book? Nobody seemed to know, and I just had to find it. I tore through the house, ripping open drawers, moving furniture, rifling through the now empty duffel bags. Babcia insisted that the cat she got rid of must have eaten it, and wasn't it a good thing he "ran away." But my cousins helped in the search, and Fela, with her sharp artist's eye, finally found it stuffed between some towels, under the bed I shared with Babcia. Who knows how it got there?

I immediately enlisted my cousins into making their contributions. Fela drew a cute little boy making eyes at an equally flirtatious little girl. Olga reminded me of my many identities, even though her poem referred only to nicknames:

You are a darling girl,
Though I don't know your name.
Are you Irusia or Kitka
Or maybe you are Terenia?
But I love you very much
My sweetest little dear
And pray that in your heart
I always will appear.

She signed it "Olga from the land of 'disgusting comedians.'"

• • • • •

May 14, 1946. The sad day arrived. Olga forbade us both to cry, but our tears blended on our wet cheeks as we held each other tight. She slipped a tiny package, wrapped in brown paper, into my palm. I unfolded the paper immediately and heard a plink as something fell to the floor. A tiny elephant, no bigger than half of my thumb, had landed smartly on his feet. He was a black lead elephant, solid and strong. His trunk proudly pointed to the sky. I lifted him tenderly.

"Elephants bring good luck," Olga said. "And they never forget. Every time you look at him, he will remind you of how much I love you."

The elephant, the autograph book, and the Virgin Mary medallion I had received at First Communion crossed the ocean in a red purse, which I never let out of my sight.

I wanted to safeguard the broken tooth, too, but my

mother insisted on carrying it herself in a cotton-filled box, like a diamond.

It was my front tooth, and it broke the day before we embarked the *Marine Perch*.

• • • • •

The ship was docked at the port of Bremen Haven. We arrived early, with a few hours to spare. It was a sunny spring day. My father suggested he and I go to the park while the ladies rested. I think he was trying to cheer me up, although actually I would have preferred to spend the time with Musia. Still, I always cherished time alone with my father.

The park featured a playground with swings and a giant seesaw. I'd never seen a seesaw before, and it looked quite intimidating. A bunch of rowdy boys were roughhousing and screaming whenever the big board tossed them up in the air.

"I'd rather go on the swings," I said to my father, giving the seesaw a wide berth.

But he wanted to treat me to a new experience. It certainly turned out to be a memorable one.

"Don't worry," he assured me, prodding me toward the contraption. "It's fun."

We waited for the boys to vacate, but they were having too good a time. My father kept glancing at his watch. We were due to go to America, after all! Finally he proposed a solution, appealing to the ruffians' honor as young gentlemen: We could share. The boys would man one end of the seesaw, and I'd sit on the other. They reluctantly agreed.

Three of them climbed aboard one end. My father pushed hard on the empty side, straining to lift the weight of three boys. The boys giggled, hanging high on their slanty perch. Their heads drooped and their knuckles turned white from grasping the board under them. My father anchored the seesaw, and I straddled my end. "Hold on," he said, and let go.

But the weight was uneven. I flew up as the heavy load at the other end banged into the ground. The collision bounced me forward and my mouth hit the board.

My father grabbed me as the boys took off, worried that they would be blamed for what had happened. The seesaw jerked back into balance.

I screamed through the whole cleanup, as my father wiped blood with his white handkerchief. Only when I stopped sobbing did I lick the inside of my swollen mouth and discover a missing front tooth. On our hands and knees my father and I scoured the sparse grass. We finally located the tooth, glued with blood to the front of my shirt. My father swaddled it in the soggy, bloody handkerchief.

It suddenly occurred to me that I had lost a permanent tooth. It wouldn't grow back like my baby teeth had.

"I'm never going to open my mouth!" I wailed. "I don't want to look like the grandpa in Mstow." And I named a few toothless residents of Neu Freiman as well.

"Don't worry," my father said. "You are not in Mstow anymore. We're going to America!" He rubbed his hands together, and his excitement trickled into me. "I bet the root is still there, and in America, the dentists work miracles.

They'll just stick the tooth back on the root and it will be as good as new."

Reassured, I smiled weakly, my tongue exploring the empty hole. A place of miracles. Maybe America would be all right after all.

●　●　●　●　●

With a throbbing gap between my teeth, I boarded the Marine Perch, a converted World War II army tub that ferried refugees from Bremen Haven to New York.

Uniformed crew members separated us by sex—women and children on deck, men below. It reminded me of the Nazi "selection" after the Warsaw Uprising. And in the manner of the "chivalrous" Nazis, the women fared better than the men.

My mother, Babcia, and I were assigned a stateroom along with seven-year-old Ninka and her mother, Rena. The room was small but airy, with a view onto the bustling deck. Ninka and I got to sleep on the top bunks and, during the first few days, we would whisper to each other and once even indulged in a pillow fight. She was too young to be much fun, but better than just grownups. Besides, my mother and Babcia spent their time gabbing with Rena. Babcia, who confided in me more than I would have wished, told me that Rena was Jewish but her husband was Polish—meaning Catholic. He drank and, when angry, which was often, would call his wife a "dirty Jew."

"Remember that, my dear," Babcia warned. "The Poles are all anti-Semites. Don't ever marry a goy."

Musia and me on the ship to America.

The men, perhaps fifty or so, were crammed together into a stifling dormitory below deck. Their portholes revealed nothing but a changeless green, like dirty glass. The dorm stank of sweat and vomit. My father was seasick throughout

Chapter 16

the journey. Occasionally Mama convinced him to climb up to the deck to breathe fresh air and throw up overboard. But he had so little energy, he preferred to stay in his narrow bunk and try to sleep. He must have lost twenty pounds in the ten days of the passage.

Ten days can be forever. Musia and I amused ourselves by making up stories about passengers who we figured did forbidden things. Musia, of course, initiated these fantasies, but I caught on pretty fast. At other times we would stagger arm in arm along the rolling deck, trying to keep our minds off the queasy feeling that would creep up on us. Neither of us actually threw up, but we often gagged. We were proud of our sea legs—or stomachs—and, in less "grownup" moments, pretended to be seasoned sailors on a pirate ship. Little Ninka followed us around, pushing to be included in our twosome. We considered her a pest, but sometimes we magnanimously allowed her to play the slave. At other times we shooed her away, and she would run complaining to her mother.

And then, one day, my annoyance with her turned into loathing.

* * * * *

The three of us are standing on the deck, counting the waves, another of our pass-the-time sports. Counting waves puts you in a trance, so we are startled by the sudden appearance on the deck of the captain himself. We figure he is on his way to the purser's office, whatever that may be (the loudspeaker is forever blaring: "So-and-So please come to the purser's office"), or to the bridge to run the ship, or to the messhall, or anywhere other than to us three insignificant kids. But he heads straight for us! He starts up a little conversation, how are we, how do we like the trip, and so on. His hands are behind his back, but when the conversation lags because we are all shy, he swings them forward and produces a package. It's wrapped in a towel. With a big flourish, he presents the thing to Ninka, the pest, as if she were a queen.

As she works at unveiling it, the captain booms an apology: "I wish I had one for each of you, but . . . well . . . I'm sure you understand . . . . Ninka is still little and you two are big girls."

All eyes are on Ninka now, and when I see what she got, I am about to die. She has dropped the towel and is cradling a beautiful doll. I haven't even seen a real doll since poor Pavelek was left in Lvov. This doll is bigger than Pavelek. She has shoulder-length, wavy golden hair, and blue eyes that open and shut, and pink porcelain cheeks. Her frilly pink dress puffs out like a dancer's. She looks like Shirley Temple, dressed for Cinderella's ball. I would give absolutely anything to have her, and right now I feel like snatching her out of that little brat's arms.

Maybe Ninka sees the glare in my eyes. In any case, without a word, not even a "thank you" to the captain, she dashes off with the doll. The captain blows me and Musia a kiss and saunters off, and I could cheerfully toss him overboard.

Musia is of no help at all. She couldn't care less.

"Aren't you too old to play with dolls?" she says with her nose up in the air. "I am."

• • • • •

That comment almost ruined our relationship, but Musia was my only friend, especially now that I totally shunned Ninka. I refused to hold the offending doll even when she offered it, and, like Musia, I pretended scorn at anyone still playing with dolls. I did sneak many envious glances, though, because of course the doll occupied a place of honor on Ninka's upper bunk.

Musia may not have sympathized, but my mother did. Maybe she never had a doll either. She lodged an angry protest with the captain. All he had to offer was another apology. Still, her effort eased my pain. And her promise:

"When we get to America . . ."

Everything will be possible in America.

• • • • •

On occasions when the waves subsided and my father's nausea gave him some relief, he would sit with me on a deck chair and engage in storytelling, his favorite activity. This time it was stories about America.

"Just wait until we get to America," he echoed my mother's sentiments one evening as we watched the sun sink into a smooth sea. "We will live in such luxury! Our table will groan under tons of delicacies, like oranges . . . ."

I knew now what an orange was and felt most sophisticated. For my birthday, three months ago, Aunt Berta had somehow obtained two of them. We shared the juicy segments eight ways, and they turned the birthday party into a festive affair.

"You think Ninka's doll is something special?" my father continued. "To tell you the truth," he whispered in a conspiratorial voice, looking around for spies, "I think she's just a rag. A nothing with nothing. Wait until you see the dolls in America! You will have the most beautiful of them all."

He watched my eyes get wide, and he suddenly shifted his tone.

"But then again," he said, his voice low, his pale face scrunching into a frown, "how can we afford these things? We don't have any money, you know." He pulled a wallet out of his pocket, like he used to pull out candy long ago. He turned it upside down and shook it. Only a couple of coins fell out. "I will not be able to work as a doctor. First I have to pass very hard exams in medicine, and they are given in English. It takes a long time to learn English."

Was this another game? Another bedtime story about princesses and monsters? Or was this the truth? My father's face betrayed no clue. I tried to blink away the tears.

"Then what will we do?" I asked, my voice trembling. A picture of Hans Christian Andersen's "Little Match Girl" flashed through my mind. I saw myself freezing in the snow, begging for alms in a tattered dress.

My father's face sprang into a smile.

"I am just joking, Kit-kit," he said gaily, rubbing his hands. "You know your daddy is smart. Learning is easy for me."

He reached into his pocket again, this time revealing the little book of English phrases that he always toted around.

"Harry is a clerk in an English bank," he declaimed proudly, pointing to the words in the book. "See? I speak English already."

I tried to decipher the strange writing: "Ha- rrr- y- ees- ah- tzlerk- een- ahn- en- gleesh bonk."

"There!" my father said approvingly. "You speak English too." He took my hand in his. "Don't worry, Kit-kit," he said. "With God's help we survived the war. As long as we're together, nothing can scare us now."

As long as we're together, I thought with a pang. We were not all together.

When the sea started rolling again and he dragged himself back to the men's pit below, I was confused and scared. What was true, and what was make-believe? Will the princess marry the prince—or will she be eaten by the monster?

On another calm afternoon, I found my parents sitting on the deck, absorbed in a large, thick book, which barely fit on my father's lap.

"It's the Neff York phone book," my mother explained, making room for me beside her. An endless list of words starting with L stared at me from the page. "Daddy wants to Americanize our name," she continued. "None of the Americans on the ship can pronounce Licht." My mother read the litany of L names, while my nearsighted father squinted at the page. She had spent her ship days learning English pronunciation.

I stifled a gush of anger. The Nazis had made us change names countless times. And now we were doing it on our own! But I rarely dared to disagree with my parents.

"Licht is the German word for light," my mother said, pointing to a series of "Lights" in the phone book. "I bet all those were Lichts before." "Light" failed to appeal to my father. Too much like Licht. My mother backed up to the Le's. "Leighton?"

"Yes, maybe Leighton," my father mused. "Or better yet, Lighton. I like that. Sounds British."

Now I got it! It wasn't about difficult pronunciation. "Licht" spelled JEW. That's why we had shed it during the war. In the Neu Freiman camp, I could be openly Jewish—while hiding my Catholic self. Were we to hide our Jewishness again in America?

"I hate Lighton," I gathered enough courage to protest. Nobody asked me why.

My father laughed.

"Don't worry," he said. "Pretty soon you'll get married. Just make sure you pick a husband whose name you like!"

●　●　●　●　●

May 24, 1946. The sea calmed down as the Marine Perch steamed into Manhattan Harbor. We leaned over the railing, my parents, Babcia, and I, our eyes darting from one sight to the next. The Statue of Liberty held her torch in the distance. Gleaming skyscrapers towered up ahead. Ships of various shapes and sizes chugged in and out of the Hudson River docks. On land, crowds were milling around.

Somewhere out there our American relatives were awaiting us. They had a boy my age. I hoped we would get along. I hoped I would not get lost in this gigantic new world.

"I don't know," Babcia said tremulously. "I'm too old for all this." Perhaps she voiced the fear we all felt.

My father stretched his arms to embrace us three generations of females under his wing.

"As long as we're together," he said.

I decided to trust him to take care of us. The loved ones I left behind slipped, for the moment, to the back of my mind. And so did the various incarnations of myself.

As Teresa (later changed to Theresa) Irena (changed to Irene) soon to be Lighton stepped onto American soil, she chose to forget:

Irena Stefania Licht, age three (and the barely known Gittle) in Katowice;

Teresa Chrystyna Urban, age six, in Przemysl and Warsaw;

Teresa Chrystyna Kaliszewska, age eight, in Mstow;

Teresa Chrystyna Teodorowicz, age nine, in Bydgoszcz;

Both Tirtza and Teresa Irena Licht, age ten, in Neu Freiman.

A curtain came down and cut me off from these little girls, Catholic and Jewish, who had been me. Perhaps my father felt something slipping from him, too, because I could have sworn that he surreptitiously crossed himself as he sauntered off the boat. I followed suit. We exchanged smiles as if we had caught each other in a naughty act.

"We're in America," he said, rubbing his hands. "*Dzieki Bogu za to.*"

"Yes, *Gott sei dank*," Babcia repeated in Yiddish, a surge of gratitude overriding her fear. Thanks be to God.

CHAPTER SEVENTEEN

. . . .

Reunion in Poland

What is life? It is the flash of a firefly.
It is the breath of a buffalo in wintertime.
It is the little shadow which runs across
the grass and loses itself in the sunset.
—Crowfoot, Blackfoot warrior

In the middle of a summer night, in 1984, I am flying to Warsaw. I want to rest so that I will be wide awake upon arrival, but the small plastic bottle of white wine on my tray fails to knock me out. I envy my daughter, Arlene, age twenty-eight, fast asleep by the window.

My neighbors across the aisle are Poles, returning to their country for the first time in twenty years. For me it's been almost forty. They are nervous; so am I—all of us unsure if it's the flight or the prospect of seeing our native land that frightens us. I try out my Polish, with limited success. For the past few weeks I have obsessed over relearning the language, clutching my "Colloquial Polish" book like a Bible. At night, half-forgotten words and phrases float through delirious dreams from which I wake exhausted.

Arlene stirs and shifts position. I'm glad she is here. Nobody else in my family wanted to come. My husband, who emigrated to the United States from Germany before the war, thought Poland would be dull and gloomy. Why not vacation in Italy? he wondered. It isn't a vacation, I explained. It's a search.

"For what?"

"For me," I said.

He didn't understand.

My parents, both in their late seventies, also declined the invitation to join me; they feared being grabbed by the police. "After all, we left illegally in 1945," they said. The fear never stops. My father waved sadly as we took off. "Find my mother's grave," he reminded me, for the umpteenth time. "And be careful."

For Arlene, the trip spells adventure—though she, too, is searching for something. Why her family is different, perhaps. As a "child of survivors," she carries her own baggage; I'm not sure what it is. Totally unfamiliar with the language, she has been bravely tackling "Polish for Travelers," tripping over tricky clumps of consonants. She has *Gdzie jest lazienka?* down pat: "Where is the bathroom?"

Language is not my only obsession. An equally daunting

problem is what presents to bring. I interrogated all my Polish-American acquaintances. Tina suggested men's BVDs, M&Ms and Starbursts, cosmetics, tea and coffee. Helena added jeans, watches, and peppercorns. Linka proposed *pieniazki*—money.

I have a suitcase full of junk. I don't know anybody's measurements. They will swim in the size 36 underwear.

Who is "they"? That question haunts me the most.

I am about to visit Marysia's sons, my Polish "brothers." Three of the four still live in various parts of Poland. Jurek, the second youngest, will meet us at the airport. I remember a round-faced, bright-eyed thirteen-year-old with a mischievous smile. What does he look like at fifty-three? Does he resemble the stuffy, red-cheeked, paunchy chef at our local Polish restaurant? Or my nervous neighbor here on the plane, across the aisle—gaunt, rotted teeth, a terrified wife with glistening gold caps? Or perhaps the handsome Polish fisherman who recently pulled me out of a jellyfish-infested lake. (Another Polish rescuer, I thought at the time.)

What about Janek, the youngest? I recall a skinny boy, serious, sad, shy. And Staszek, the oldest, already a man of seventeen when I arrived on his doorstep in 1943. The prospect of seeing Staszek scares me; I don't think he liked me much. I will not see the fourth brother. Zbyszek disappeared right after the war. He never told his family where he was. It has been a painful mystery to his brothers.

Who are they now? And who am I? A Jew returning to the mass grave of my people. I feel defensive. On the connecting flight from Frankfurt to Warsaw, I strike up a conversation with two men in clerical garb. One is a young American priest, delighted to find himself seated with the bishop from Lublin. The young priest urges me to visit churches. "I am returning to see the people who rescued me during the Holocaust," I say. They get the point: JEWISH! The bishop claims that he "never would have guessed." Most Jews have "longer, sharper noses." He smiles benevolently—apparently he means this as a compliment. He tells me about a Jewish boy hidden during the war in a monastery. The boy became a priest and now ministers to Christian wives of Polish Jews in Israel. This unique solution to the "Jewish problem" gratifies the bishop.

We touch ground to general applause, a tribute to the pilot. Machine guns, manned by stony-faced guards, point straight at us as we disembark. In 1984, communism is still alive and well in Poland, and the authorities view travelers from the United States as a threat. We pass muster and take our first steps into the country that gave me life—and almost took it away.

The cold shiver engendered by the gun-slinging welcoming committee dissipates as my eyes turn to the gallery overlooking the arrival area. Scores of waiting friends and relatives crowd at the railing, scanning the passengers. Bent under heavy airline bags and assorted gifts picked up in Frankfurt during our stopover there, Arlene and I stumble across the guarded outdoor field toward the airport terminal. We crane our necks to search the smiling faces in the gallery above. We search for the face that my daughter has seen only in a few old photos and that I last saw when I was six. I can't find him, and for a moment I think perhaps I made him up, made up a childhood in Poland, complete with a child who never existed.

Inside the terminal, we breeze through customs. "What did you bring?" asks the customs official. I count off the gift items: underwear, M&Ms, etc. He stops me with "I see you have nothing," and waves me on.

Suddenly Arlene has dropped her luggage and is hugging Jurek, because of course it is Jurek and of course they recognize each other, although they have never met. And what I see is a spunky boy hugging my daughter, for to me he is still thirteen, though his waist has thickened and his hair has thinned. It is the smile, the crooked, mischievous smile that has remained unchanged. And his mother's soft green eyes, "our" mother's gentle eyes. I am grateful that her eyes have survived in him, because Marysia is in the cemetery, and all I can do is visit her there.

Visiting the living among my "rescue" family and visiting the dead: Those are the basic goals of this trip. My paternal grandmother's grave. She died before the war. Those who died during the war have no graves. Those who died after the war did not include Jews. But Marysia lies in the cemetery, and so does her mother, Kasia.

I wonder what Jurek is seeing as he looks at me now, the "little princess" who stole his mother, who plunged his family into danger during those monstrous years of the war. What is going through his mind as he stretches out his arms toward that child standing here with wrinkles, dyed hair, and a grown daughter? Jurek and his brothers knew that little girl during the war years when her own family was far away. Only they can attest to the fact that she existed, that she cried and laughed, that she was real.

But after the first set of hugs and greetings, there is little time for wondering. Jurek grabs our suitcases and heaves them into a waiting car. His English is passable. We try out both languages, each wanting to practice the other. I am glad for Arlene's sake that English will be used, and pleased with my ability to maneuver in Polish after all these years.

"Where are we going?" Arlene asks as the overloaded car jerks to a start.

"Everywhere you want," Jurek replies. "For the next three weeks I am at your service."

What I want is to see the maze of hiding places that sheltered me during the war. And most of all, I want to see my other two brothers. Jurek promises a family reunion in Przemysl, the city where we lived together all those years ago.

We had much ground to cover before the family reunion.

* * * * *

Speeding through the congested city streets, Jurek pointed with pride to rebuilt Warsaw, a phoenix risen from the ashes. To me, the Communist-inspired blockhouses looked plain, colorless, and depressing. Big store windows displayed very few goods. A long line of waiting customers snaked behind a shipment of watermelons. More interesting to me were the outskirts of town, where the thick forests stirred childhood memories of picking mushrooms, wild strawberries, and tart red currants.

"Russian tanks are hidden behind those trees," Jurek informed us, breaking the magic spell.

Our first destination was the convent on whose doorstep I had arrived at the age of seven. Jurek pulled to a stop. "Where in the world is Belvederska Street?" he frowned, squinting at the map. A resident of Bialystok, he was not very familiar with Warsaw streets. Also, although a full professor of education, he shriveled before maps.

"I'll ask somebody," he decided. "Excuse me, sir . . ." he shouted out the window at the first passerby.

A bald man approached and pointed us in the right direction. He seemed to find an affinity with Jurek and, before moving on, proceeded to treat him to a joke:

"Did you hear the one about the two guys who got into an argument? The first one threatens: 'If you keep this up, I'm gonna beat your Jew.' 'Oh, yeah,' the other guy retorts, 'if you beat my Jew, I'm gonna beat your Jew.'"

The raconteur chuckled companionably and reached through the window to clap Jurek on the shoulder. Noticing me and Arlene, he acknowledged us with a friendly wave of the hand. Jurek ignored the "joke" and stepped on the gas. A chilling introduction to 1980's Poland. Anti-Semitism lives on, I thought, despite a forty-year absence of Jews.

I recognized Belvederska, a spacious boulevard, tree lined, with large homes set well back from the street behind gray walls. We again stopped for directions, this time to the convent.

"Oh, it used to be over here," a woman carrying two bags of groceries said, "but the Russians demolished what was left of it. They built their embassy across the street and didn't want to be looking at a Catholic institution every day!"

She suggested that we check out Swietego Kazimierza Church, where a few nuns had moved after the war. We might find some information there.

The gate of the church led into a garden, where an emaciated man was trimming the roses. He said there was one sister around who had lived in a convent during the German occupation. He didn't know which convent.

"Sister Odona is out visiting the sick, but she never misses lunch," he laughed, flashing one lone tooth. "You are welcome to wait for her here."

An hour later, an elderly nun appeared. She wore a gray habit; the sisters I remember had worn black. She was clearly from a different convent. Nevertheless, she seemed pleased by our visit and the opportunity to share her own story.

"We saved many children in our orphanage," she said. "And a number of them were Jewish."

The Germans mostly left the convents alone, she told us, and so she wasn't afraid of them. "Sometimes I would scold them like little boys," Sister Odona said. "Of course we never revealed that we were hiding Jewish children," she added. "Even most of our sisters didn't know. We could trust only a few."

Sister Odona paused to collect her memories. "No," she went on, in something of a conspiratorial tone. "I wasn't afraid to help the Jews." She related going to execution sites to offer condemned Jews consolation and a chance to convert. "Those who accepted Christ at the last moment were saved and their souls went directly, *prosciutko*, to heaven," she explained.

I recalled my own efforts to achieve salvation before death and pictured Sister Odona giving the dying Jews what I had once wanted for myself. But my views of life had changed since then, and now the image distressed me.

* * * * *

We spent the evening with Jurek's cousins. They lived in Stare Miasto, Warsaw's "Old City," which has been reconstructed to duplicate the beautiful, original medieval town. Their apartment was small but lovely, with very high ceilings, a balcony, lots of light. It was sparsely furnished, with old Persian carpets, a worn-out couch, a rickety lamp, two TVs. The kitchen made up in atmosphere what it lacked in modern conveniences: Homemade garlic pickles were marinating in jars on the floor; mushrooms hung on a string to dry; a giant jar of fermenting sour cherries stood waiting to be pressed into wisniak, a cherry wine.

The goodwill engendered by a hearty dinner and plentiful liquor withered a bit as the cousins' daughter, a young physician, confronted Arlene and me with a challenge.

"I think the American view of Poland is totally unfair."

She had read an article, written in the United States, that accused Poles of accomplishing after the war what the Germans had failed to do: They had made Poland, according to this author, *Juden Frei*, "free of Jews."

"That's just a lie," the young woman bristled. "There are plenty of Jews still in Poland."

I didn't know how to respond. It was common knowledge that anti-Zionist demonstrations, firings from responsible jobs, and even pogroms had occurred in Poland following the 1967 Six-Day War in Israel. The Communists sided with the Arabs in that conflict, and Jews were labeled the enemy. A massive exodus out of Poland of most surviving Jews occurred within the next few months.

"Many Jews are thriving here in business and the professions," another of the cousins chipped in. "Of course most have converted and intermarried, but that just makes sense to do for your career."

The young doctor said, "We also get blamed for not helping Jews during the war. And that, too, is a lie. Helping was common, rather than unusual. It was done matter-of-factly, without much thought. Someone needed help, so you helped. My parents helped." She turned toward her parents, who nodded but did not join the discussion. "Often many people were involved in rescuing one family, or one Jew," she went on, "like in moving the person from house to house, maybe even for one night at a time."

The young woman's reproach seemed to split us into "we" and "they"—the Poles and the Jews. Hurt, anger, guilt, blame, on both sides. The wounds still gape open.

The young woman looked me straight in the eye.

"Please share what I have told you with the people in America," she asked.

•　•　•　•　•

It was a raw, rainy day as we wended our way toward Auschwitz, the site of the infamous death camp. The pastoral scenery—cows, haystacks, horse-and-buggies, geese—seemed out of place on this trip to hell. Arlene and I, independently, focused entirely on our destination. Did the people who had lived along this rustic road during the war see the transports? Did they know what was happening here? How many Germans were needed to search through all these cozy little houses? Did any of them shelter Jews? Did the Jews hide from house to house, like Jurek's cousin had asserted? In the haylofts? In the fields? Were these the tracks that carried the trains?

Jurek seemed free of such somber thoughts, and he chattered cheerfully about this and that.

The town of Auschwitz shocked me even more than the peaceful scenery leading up to it. Auschwitz, on this day, was bubbling with merriment: balloons, carousel rides, a Ferris wheel—a laughing, ice-cream-licking crowd. A carnival. I had to shift into a different mindset in order to allow the modern-day citizens of Auschwitz the right to play.

Even more surreal was the sight of the death camp itself, with a hotel and signs of residence on its very grounds. Inside the entrance, visitors were buying colorful dolls and other local crafts in a souvenir shop. The smell of weak coffee reached us from a cafeteria. Arlene and I couldn't imagine shopping or, worst of all, sleeping here. We did have to use the toilet and even that seemed sacrilegious.

On our way back from the camp, not a word was spoken. Words were not designed for this.

• • • • •

The weather had cleared a bit when we pulled into Krakow. I'd never been there before, but we wanted to make a brief stop in this stately, and undestroyed, city. Parking the car, we strolled through the "Planty Gardens," which had been off limits to Jews even early during the war. But suddenly the skies opened up again and we ducked into the nearest church: the magnificent Mariacka. Jurek wanted to show us the famous altar, but when he realized that a mass was in progress, he turned to leave. I was amazed to learn that he refused to participate in Catholic rituals. The Church, he told us, was a regressive force, causing increasing problems for the country.

"More and more churches are being built," he grumbled, "when what we need is more schools."

Unspoken was the fact that Jurek feared being seen in a church. Under the Communist regime, such a thing could have cost him his university job. But I wanted to stay; already in the doorway, a rush of familiarity had washed over me. Jurek offered to wait in the lobby.

Entering by a side door, Arlene and I could not see the altar, but we heard the priest's voice, the organ music, and the answering chorus of the massive congregation. And everywhere I saw Marysia. She was carried in the arms of Jesus, whose pictures ascended higher and higher toward the ornate ceiling. She was blossoming among bountiful white lilies. She was kneeling amidst the congregation. She was walking into the church, holding the hand of a child. She was in heaven with the saints. Her face was the face of the Virgin. I longed, more than anything, to tell her I loved her and I prayed to who- or whatever in that church had the power to send her that message. Marysia, what would you say if you saw your little Jewish Tereska praying in Mariacka Church, and your Jurek pacing the hall outside?

• • • • •

We were almost ready for Przemysl, but we had to make one more stop.

Mstow, the farm village to which the Germans deported us after the Warsaw Uprising, had not changed at all. I recognized the imposing church on the hill, right outside the gate to the town. The little bridge still crossed the river, the tiny pastel huts still hid their inner courtyards, the little park still graced the center of the town square. The same gaggle of old men still sat around on the two park benches. And the same group of local citizens was still gathered in front of the practically empty card shop. We approached them.

"Were any of you around in 1944?" we asked, "right after the Warsaw Uprising?"

An old lady nodded, but she'd only heard about the Uprising; it was far away. No she didn't remember the refugees who had come here. A thin, dark, unshaven, withered man volunteered that he had been a child at the time. It turned out that we had been born within days of each other. We must have gone to school together! Looking at him, I thought gratefully that the years had been kinder to me. My schoolmate agreed to pose for a picture, and pretty soon the whole group smiled into the camera.

Leaving our new friends behind, we waved down an old peasant clattering down a cobblestone alley, straddling an empty hay cart. He reluctantly pulled on the reins of his bony horse. We asked if we could take his picture. The peasant looked frightened, suspicious, allowing the picture "if it's necessary." Goodness knows who he thought we were! No, he didn't remember 1944. It was long ago. He shook the reins and took off.

And so time had stood still in Mstow. The people remembered what they chose to remember, and they kept to themselves. The winding streets were peaceful, and I could see why I had loved this town so, after the hell of the Warsaw Uprising.

* * * * *

Przemysl. How to describe the reunion?

Janek, who still lived there, was our host. He threw open the door as we rang the doorbell. I was surprised at his girth, a big difference from the slim boy I remembered. He kissed me and Arlene on the hand, in old-fashioned style, then planted three kisses on our cheeks. Slinging my heavy suitcase over his shoulder, he laughed that he used to lug me around that way all over Przemysl. My oldest brother, Staszek, now appeared, as massive as Janek and much friendlier than I had expected. He too distributed kisses and ushered us into Janek's living room, where other family members had gathered. These included primarily wives and grown children

Sharing family photos with my brothers, 1984.

of my three brothers. Arlene gravitated toward Ewa, Jurek's older daughter, who had just finished medical school. They were the same age and managed to communicate across the language barrier. It thrilled me to see the relationship of our two families continuing to grow.

The walls were lined with old photographs that immediately brought tears to my eyes, because some of the faces in the pictures were no longer here. Zbyszek was so conspicuously absent from the group of the brothers. And, most important, Marysia. She was missing, but her spirit filled the room. Jurek put his arm around me, and I felt so full and yet so empty at the same time. A hole where Marysia should have been.

Noting my interest in photographs, Janek pulled out his picture album.

"Here is our family," he said, "and you are part of it."

Indeed, there I was, age five. Janek unglued whatever pictures appealed to me the most. My favorite was of Marysia and me, our arms about each other. Staszek, pointing to his ample stomach, indicated that it was time to eat.

The table was sumptuously set, with several types of ham and kielbasa, herring, fresh bread and butter, cucumbers and tomatoes. This obviously represented a major financial outlay, and judging by Janek's simple lodging, he was no millionaire.

We broke out the Scotch that I had brought and added it to the large bottle of Vodka Wyborowa. The "boys" began to sing, with Janek, the music teacher, leading with an iron hand. I was five again. They were treating me like their little sister-princess, vying for my attention, serenading me. It was a long-forgotten warm bath.

We talked, too, of course. I posed my big question: Why did you shelter a strange Jewish child at such risk to yourselves? There were many answers—and not really any.

Marysia had always wanted a daughter. "I was supposed to be it," Jurek, the third in sibling order, said. "We boys liked to be big heroes and show off for you," Staszek laughed. No, they weren't jealous, they insisted, though somehow I had a different impression. All in all, my question was basically avoided. They just did it, that's all, and now let me know they loved me.

· · · · ·

The next day, we visited graves. We all gathered at the Catholic cemetery. Janek led the way through the hilly, park-like grounds. Beautifully maintained graves, full of flowers. The family grave housed the remains of Marysia; her mother, Kasia; her sister, Zosia; and her husband, Jozef. I thought about my father and how moved he would be to see these four names together. For me, though, the experience was bland. I didn't feel Marysia's presence here.

Jurek now proposed that we look for my grandmother's grave. We asked directions to the Jewish cemetery, and an obliging couple offered to escort us. An overgrown, grassy field was separated from the Catholic cemetery by chicken wire. We followed our guides through a hole in the fence and waded up a hill, through rampant weeds. Suddenly we found ourselves in front of a broken tombstone, standing askew, one of its corners dug deep into the earth. We saw a few other scattered stones, barely perceptible through the weeds, and almost tripped on a rocky fragment. Our guides walked on ahead and then returned to us with information:

There's a keeper for this Jewish cemetery, name of Shlomko. He will have records, a register. He might know if my grandmother's grave can be found. I wanted to forget the whole thing, but Jurek insisted that we search out the keeper. Jurek is, at heart, a historian.

Shlomko was a short man in his seventies, clean-shaven. He was shabbily dressed but otherwise looked no different than a synagogue elder in America. He welcomed our offer to confer in a coffee shop. Arlene, Jurek, and I took him in tow, while the couple who had guided us went on their way.

Shlomko refused coffee and tea, but his face lit up at the suggestion of cake. He ate with gusto, pulling out photos of his daughter in America and the grandchildren. He'd been to the States for a few months, but felt that everyone there was just interested in business. Besides, it didn't agree with his health. He felt better in Poland.

It took several tries to direct Shlomko's attention to the subject at hand. No, there isn't any register, there's nothing. Nobody but he cares about the cemetery, not in Poland, nor abroad. He returned to the pictures of his family, eager to share the living part of his existence. "So is there a cemetery?" we pressed. He reluctantly agreed to take us there, and we all climbed into Jurek's car.

The entrance was on the other side of the field that we had seen earlier. Shlomko donned a yarmulke and pulled out keys to unlock the chain holding the gate. We saw a somewhat cleared area with three good-size stones. The center one was a memorial to Jews murdered by the Nazis. The other two were tombstones of Przemysl citizens who had died in the early 1970s. The majority of the five hundred or so Jews who had remained in Przemysl after World War II had left in the late '60s, chased away by anti-Zionist demonstrations.

How many are still left? Shlomko wrinkled his forehead in thought. Well, there's Mrs. R on the other side of town, and he thought old Mrs. G was still around. Yes, there were another two. Four Jews in all, besides himself. The others, he added, almost as an afterthought, have all converted. Recent burials have taken place in the Catholic cemetery.

We looked beyond the three showpiece memorials and saw that only a few tombstones had been cleared of weeds. We trudged through the thick undergrowth searching for signs of Gizela Licht, my grandmother. Her Jewish name had been Gittle—my Jewish name, too. It was a hopeless cause. We gave Shlomko some money with a request to either try to find her grave, or, at least, to clear off a couple of others.

It was with considerable difficulty that we were able to dislodge Shlomko from our car, as he obviously wanted to stay as long as possible. He asked me several times if I was Jewish, for some reason not believing that this was really true. As we drove away, I felt sad leaving this man—a lonely, partly senile Jew, one of the sole survivors of the once thriving Jewish community of Przemysl.

* * * * *

The next day, all three brothers took us sightseeing. First stop: Podsanie, the part of Przemysl on the banks of the river San. Our house had stood right on this riverfront. We headed for it. My brothers had not been here for almost as long as I. At first I didn't recognize it: a three-story villa, quite impressive, with the name Wila Jadwiga engraved in large letters across the top. It didn't begin to look familiar until we made our way to the back, a shabby, peeling facade strung with clotheslines. Children were playing in the backyard, which had seemed bigger when we were young. Staszek pointed out the adjoining house—the Gestapo headquarters at the time. Zbyszek used to clean for them and once got into trouble for playing the Polish national anthem on their piano.

"How did you ever survive, with the Gestapo next door?" Arlene wondered.

"It's always darkest right under the lamp," Jurek replied.

●　　●　　●　　●　　●

The broad, if littered, promenade along the river was lined with benches and stone chess tables. Women in babushkas sat there discussing their problems, while groups of men and children played chess. Janek, who had taught music here for years, was in his element. Gentlemen greeted him, bowing formally. A former student, wheeling a moon-faced baby with a pointed bonnet, stopped to show off the child.

"I'm not bragging, but I do have a certain status in this town," Janek said shyly. And I was glad to witness it.

Down by the river, more memories. The boys used to swim, bathe, wash clothes in it. Once Marysia sent Jurek down with the laundry and he lost half of it in the current. Another time, the river claimed his boots.

Leaving the river, we moved on to the castle. It stands on

a hill in a pleasant park. We played here as children, the boys carrying me on their shoulders. My brothers pointed out various landmarks, the statue with its head now knocked off, the chestnut trees. We all easily slipped back to our childhoods, romping over the hills, climbing the walls surrounding the castle. There were some carefree moments in those years, I thought, for which I have to thank this family.

Back for dinner in Janek's apartment, we found the table again beautifully set and platters of ham, cheese, and canned sprats overflowing. In between singing and talking, Janek apologized for the cold meals and the sooty walls. The stove had broken several weeks ago. The house had filled with smoke while he slept. He barely got out alive.

I looked at my three brothers, grateful that I came when I did. They were no longer young—and neither was I. Staszek, obese and addicted to cigarettes, had a heart condition. Janek, also obese and given to drink, having just stopped smoking after a bout with angina, almost was asphyxiated in the fire. Jurek had spent time in a sanatorium for heart and stomach problems.

We returned to Warsaw for our flight back. Several family members accompanied us to the airport. As we waved goodbye, tears rolled down my face. Who knew if we would ever see one another again? But my heart was full. In addition to the grown daughter whom I had brought with me, I was taking home a small child—the little girl who had spent forty years hiding in the rubble of the past.

By now, I have traveled to Poland several more times, introducing my younger daughter, Debora, and my second husband, Gerald, to the Niemiec family. My son, Jeffrey, and his wife, Lili, will join me next. The trips have not been one-sided; Jurek and his son have visited us in the United States.

Getting to know the wives, children, and grandchildren of my brothers has been a delight for me. I am thrilled that the loving connection between the Niemiec family and mine, having started at the beginning of the twentieth century with my father's wet-nurse, Kasia, now stretches into the fourth generation.

My parents never got back to Poland. They and Babcia stayed together in New York for many healthy years. My mother, now in her nineties, still forms the warm center around which our family often gathers.

As for my father, he continued telling stories as long as he lived. Perhaps I have inherited his role. The storyteller's task is to pass on to the next generation those events that must be remembered.

POSTSCRIPT

In 1988, Maria (Marysia) and Jozef Niemiec were awarded Israel's Medal of the Righteous of the Nations. It is inscribed:

HE WHO SAVES ONE LIFE IS CONSIDERED
AS SAVING THE WHOLE UNIVERSE.

A plaque in their honor has been placed at the Yad Vashem Holocaust Memorial in Jerusalem.

ACKNOWLEDGMENTS

In the creation of this book, I have been helped by many individuals. Lisa Clyde Nielsen, the world's best editor, lent her sharp eye and gentle touch to endless revisions. Sonja Glassman artistically designed the book and, in collaboration with Calico Harington, performed the necessary computer magic. I thank Dorcas Gelabert for designing the cover and my agent, Wendy Schmalz, for her unfailing encouragement and optimism.

For the current UNM Press paperback edition, I am grateful to Kristie Miller for bringing *Hide and Seek* to the attention of Editor in Chief and Associate Director, David Holtby. Thank you, David, for your enthusiastic reception and for guiding me patiently through the details of the publication process. Thanks to artist Robyn Mundy for the beautiful new cover and interior design, and to Managing

Editor Evelyn Schlatter, as well as to the rest of the UNM Press staff for all their hard work and expert craftsmanship. My writers' "cuddle-group" offered continuous support and invaluable criticism at every stage of the book's gestation. The group included Betty Christie, Kim Feltes, Maria Elena Gonzales, Liz Jones, Karol Nielsen, Martha Mortensen and Walteen Truly. Bill Black and Adam Sexton, of the Gotham writing school, were my mentors in the craft of producing a memoir.

I am grateful to my Polish "brothers," Jurek and Staszek Niemiec, for guiding me along the roads of Poland, as well as the often foggy lanes of memory. Their reminiscences, and also those of my mother, Elizabeth Lighton, enriched and complemented my own.

Thanks to my children—Arlene and Michael Gordon, Jeffrey Cahn and Lili Schad, and Debora Cahn—for both substantive and emotional assistance. The book is, first and foremost, for them. And special thanks to my husband, Gerald Tober, for his ever-ready helping hand and loving heart.

Finally, I want to take this opportunity to express my deep appreciation to the readers of the first edition, many of whom took the trouble to share with me their heartfelt and moving reactions to *Hide and Seek*.